Coming of Age
HAVAMAL

A New Translation
For Young Heathens

Carrie Overton

The Coming of Age Havamal

© 2020 Carrie Overton

ISBN: 978-1-937571-47-4

Cover Image: ©H. Koppdelaney

https://creativecommons.org/licenses/by-nd/2.0/legalcode

Huginn & Muninn Publishing

www.huginnandmuninn.net

This book is dedicated to my children
Runa, Heidi & Wulfric

May the wisdom of Odin and the virtues
of the Havamal inspire you to strive always
toward personal excellence.

*"One thing I know that never dies is the fame
of each man's deeds"*

With all my love,
Mom

INTRODUCTION

This book is for Heathens who are embarking on one of the most important changes in their lives, their *Coming of Age*.

What does it mean to Come of Age?

Coming of Age is the recognition that a person has left childhood and entered adulthood. This means they are no longer treated as a child but rather as an adult who is capable of caring for themselves and is fully responsible for their own life.

In most ancient cultures this process was one of the most important turning point in a person's life. This process was often marked by a rite of passage; a ritual that recognized that they have left childhood behind and are fully accepted in the community. Unfortunately in our recent history this important recognition of self-reliance has been lost. There is no defined point where a person becomes an adult and is expected to fully care for themselves.

This is one of the reasons why people feel so lost and unsure of their purpose as they grow in our culture today. In recent times it has become more and more common for people who are far into their adult age to continue living with their parents and be provided for by their parents.

There is nothing wrong with living with your family. Indeed this is how our ancestors lived in tribes in ancient times. However, if you lived with your family it was a fact that you as the younger adult took over the responsibility of caring for older family members, not the other way around.

The problem with how young people are regarded today is that they are not expected to know what it means to be an adult. They are not encouraged that doing what adults do is the right thing for them and will bring them the happiness and confidence they need for the rest of their lives, so they do not grow fully into adulthood, nor do they take on all the responsibilities that go along with being an adult. This is a great disservice to young people. It leads them to hopelessness, depression, a lack of purpose, and often ends in self-destructive behavior like drug use or alcohol abuse.

This book is for young people who are ready to take on the responsibility of becoming an adult. Young people who are seeking to establish their self-reliance. To prove to themselves, to their family and the greater community that they are ready to stand on their own two feet and become full members of the community. To be regarded as an equal among adults.

This is not an easy task to achieve but one that is necessary for all of us to complete if we are to live our lives with confidence while we follow the path our ancestors have laid out for us.

Why take on this task when so many around you are not? Because if you do, you will be in a better position in life than they are. You will not be tricked by those who would attempt to sway you heart and mind to their own benefit. You will grow into a fully realized and ideal person. You will not feel the need to compare yourself with or try to emulate others because you will have a solid understanding of who you are.

How do I Come of Age?

Within this book you will read the Words of Odin a collection of wisdom passed down by our ancestors that tell us how to do well in life and not bring shame upon ourselves or our family. It gives us the Morals and Virtues we need to guide us to adulthood and through our entire lives.

These morals and virtues are not something made up recently to match a political or social trend. They are pieces of wisdom that have been passed down from grandparents and parents to their children and grandchildren for thousands of years. It was only recently when this ancestral knowledge was cut off from us. But you can rise to the challenge and reclaim it. For yourself, for your children and for your children's children.

In these pages you will see what it takes to not only become an adult but to be the best person you can be your whole life through. To our ancestors and to the reawakening spirit of Heathens today, there are two things in our lives that matter most. To be remembered by our children and to be remember as a wise and noble person.

What are Morals and Virtues?

Morals are knowing what behaviors are right and wrong. Virtues are when you take the morals you have learned and act in the right way.

When you live a life of virtue you not only become an adult, but also grow into a wise and noble person who is worthy of respect from your family and community.

As you read this book you will see on the page opposite the Havamal stanza there is page which will allow you to add your own thoughts. As well as write down what you think the moral is within the words and which virtue you think would match those morals.

This book is just one stepping stone along your path toward Excellence. I will leave you now to begin your journey with Odin's words:

> "I give you this advice, accept my guidance
> and it will benefit you if you heed it"

The Coming of Age
HAVAMAL

1. Before going into a room look at every door and throughout the entire place. Pay attention and be aware of who is present.
Could there be people who want to do you harm?

My Thoughts

_____
_____
_____
_____
_____
_____
_____
_____

The Moral

_____
_____
_____
_____
_____

The Virtue

_____
_____

2. When a guest comes to your home,
make him comfortable, give him food,
warmth and good conversation.
You do not know what he has endured
before coming to visit.

My Thoughts

_____
_____
_____
_____
_____
_____
_____
_____

The Moral

_____
_____
_____
_____
_____

The Virtue

_____
_____

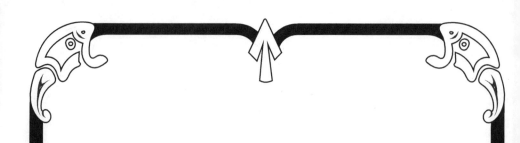

3. A guest who has traveled far needs to be well taken care of.
Make sure they are comfortable.
Offer them food, a shower, fresh clothing, a warm place to relax and a nice bed to sleep in.

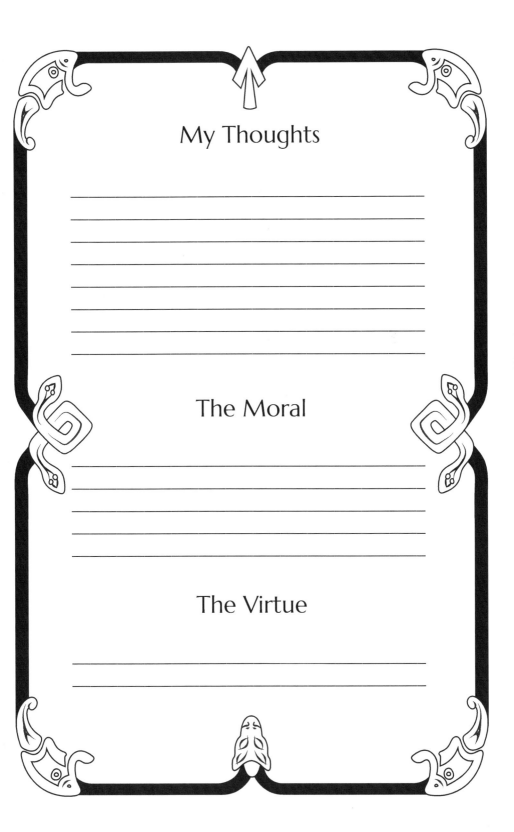

My Thoughts

_____
_____
_____
_____
_____
_____
_____
_____

The Moral

_____
_____
_____
_____

The Virtue

_____
_____

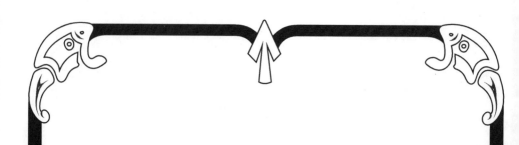

4. When a guest comes your responsibility is to make them feel welcome with kind words and to provide for his needs. Your guests responsibility is to give you enjoyable company and good conversation as well.

My Thoughts

_____
_____
_____
_____
_____
_____
_____
_____

The Moral

_____
_____
_____
_____
_____

The Virtue

_____
_____

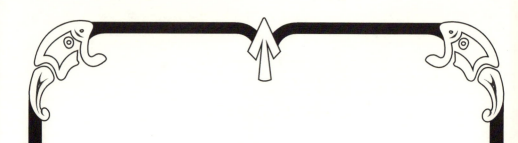

5. If you are going to leave home and experience more of the world you must have a good understanding of common sense. Use your wisdom and speak only when you have thought well about your words.

If you speak without thinking, those wiser than you will think you are weak and those more cunning will take advantage of you.

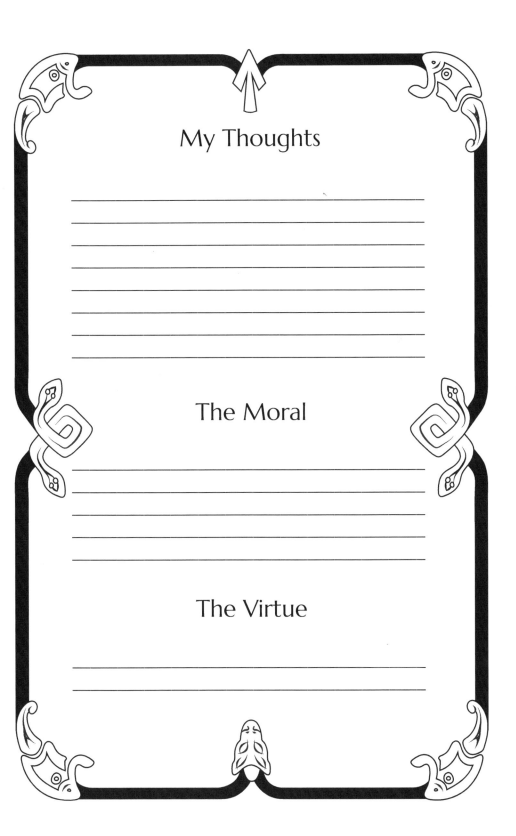

My Thoughts

_____
_____
_____
_____
_____
_____
_____
_____

The Moral

_____
_____
_____
_____
_____

The Virtue

_____
_____

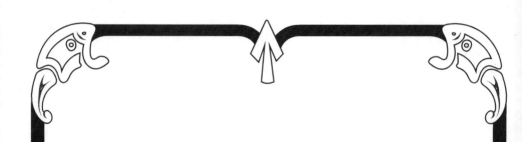

6. Even if you are very wise you should never boast about your intelligence. Rather be silent and careful with your words.
Speak only what you must when you are around people who are not kin*.
Let your words be strong and to the point. Harm usually comes to those who speak too much.

Kin: Your family, your tribe.

My Thoughts

_____
_____
_____
_____
_____
_____
_____
_____

The Moral

_____
_____
_____
_____

The Virtue

_____
_____

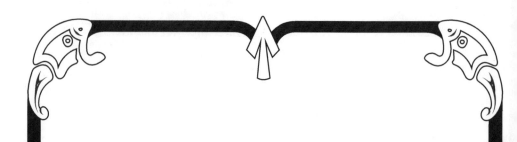

7. When you are a guest among strangers be silent and pay attention.
Listen well with your ears and look closely with your eyes.
This is what the wisest do when in a strange place and the easiest way to avoid most harm.

My Thoughts

_____
_____
_____
_____
_____
_____
_____
_____

The Moral

_____
_____
_____
_____
_____

The Virtue

_____
_____

8. Be happy with yourself.
Strive to be the best you can be.
When you are confident and just*
toward others, you will be well liked and
people will speak nicely of you.
However, do not rely on the words of
others to give you confidence.
Many times weak people will try to
convince you that you are not as wise or
not as good as you are.

Just: To be reasonable, to behave and think using fact,
reason, logic and rationality.

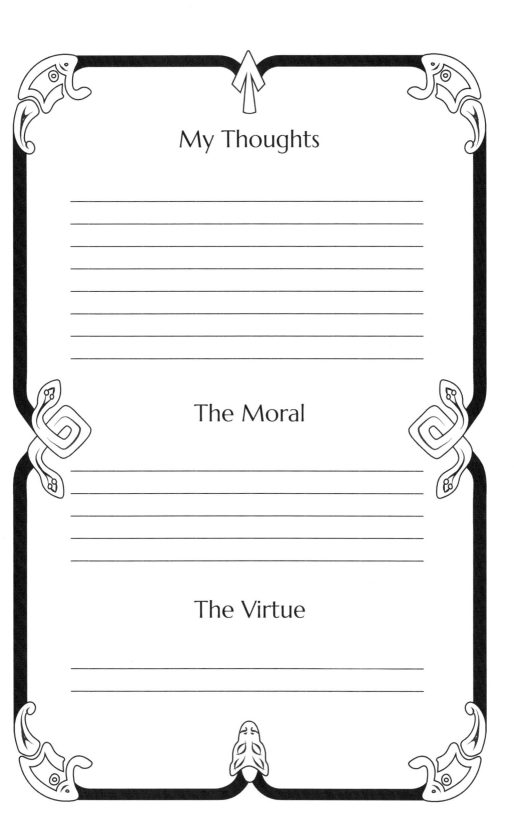

My Thoughts

_____
_____
_____
_____
_____
_____
_____
_____

The Moral

_____
_____
_____
_____
_____

The Virtue

_____
_____

9. You will be happy throughout your life if you trust in your common sense.
Always question the intentions of what other people tell you to believe.
Often times they do not have your best interests in mind.

My Thoughts

_____
_____
_____
_____
_____
_____
_____
_____

The Moral

_____
_____
_____
_____

The Virtue

_____
_____

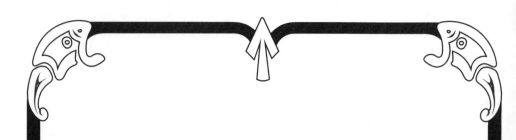

10. The one thing that will guide you best in life is your own strong common sense. When you are sad it will bring you comfort. Well trained, your own critical wisdom is better than any amount of money in the world.

Rich or poor, *Mother's Wit matters most.

What is Mother's Wit?

Mother's Wisdom: From a young age our mothers tell us these things. "Don't hit your sister." "Don't stand too close to that cliff." "Stay away from strangers." These are only a few examples of things we should know are wrong or dangerous as we grow out of early childhood. Mother's Wit refers to the instinctual wisdom we carry with us. Things that we know are right or wrong because we can sense that it is. Mother's Wit is a well developed common sense.

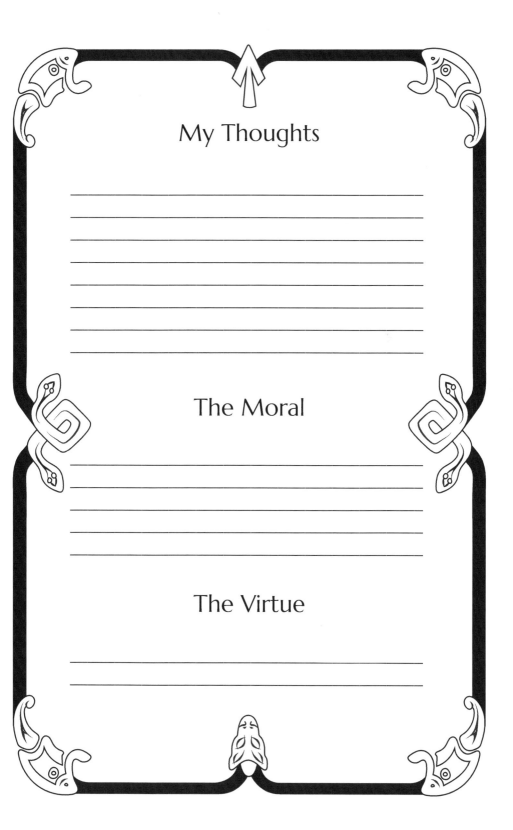

My Thoughts

_____
_____
_____
_____
_____
_____
_____

The Moral

_____
_____
_____
_____
_____

The Virtue

_____
_____

11. The most important thing to have when you travel is your wisdom.
The worst thing you could do is drink too much alcohol and lose your wits.

My Thoughts

_____
_____
_____
_____
_____
_____
_____
_____

The Moral

_____
_____
_____
_____
_____

The Virtue

_____
_____

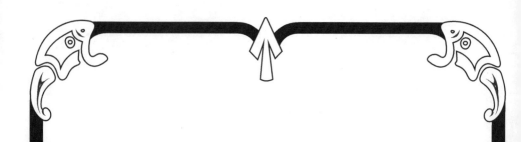

12. By hearing the words of weak people it may seem that drinking a lot of alcohol is ok.
However these same people drink too much and lose all of their Common Sense. It is better to have only a few drinks on occasion and keep your wits about you.

My Thoughts

_____
_____
_____
_____
_____
_____
_____
_____

The Moral

_____
_____
_____
_____

The Virtue

_____
_____

13. When people drink too much alcohol they forget to hold their tongue* and their common sense vanishes.
Foolish I became when with Gunnlod* I was drinking.

Hold Your Tongue: This is a figure of speech that means you stop talking or be quiet. To illustrate it. If you grab your tongue and hold it tight you will not be able to speak anymore will you?
Why is it important to know when to Hold Your Tongue (be quiet)?

Read the story of The Mead of Poetry if you would like to know more about Odin and Gunnlod.

My Thoughts

_____
_____
_____
_____
_____
_____
_____

The Moral

_____
_____
_____
_____
_____

The Virtue

_____
_____

14. Foolishly I was too drunk when at cunning Fjalar's hall I drank.
Happy I was when afterward my wits finally came back to me.
Don't drink too much, you will do and say things you would not normally do and make yourself look foolish.

Read the story of The Mead of Poetry if you would like to know more about Odin and Gunnlod.

My Thoughts

_____
_____
_____
_____
_____
_____
_____

The Moral

_____
_____
_____
_____

The Virtue

_____
_____

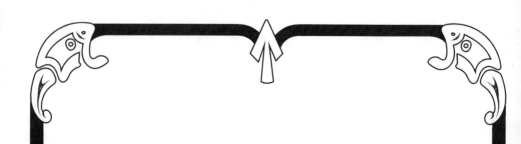

15. Silent and wise should one with strong character be, who seeks excellence in life. Knowing how to act bravely in difficult situations and crisis is also a trait of the strong.
Be joyful and generous until the day you die.

My Thoughts

_____
_____
_____
_____
_____
_____
_____
_____

The Moral

_____
_____
_____
_____
_____

The Virtue

_____
_____

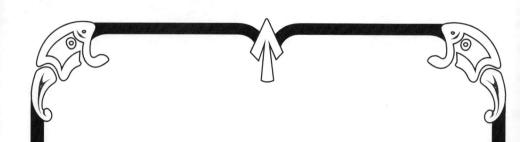

16. A coward thinks he will live forever if he hides away from anything he thinks could harm him.
But he too will die one day just as we all do.

My Thoughts

_____
_____
_____
_____
_____
_____
_____

The Moral

_____
_____
_____
_____
_____

The Virtue

_____
_____

17. A Fool stares wide eyed when he goes to gathering, keeping to himself, he mopes and speaks quietly so others cannot hear him when he is asked questions.
But give him alcohol and suddenly he speaks too much without saying anything important at all.

My Thoughts

_____
_____
_____
_____
_____
_____
_____
_____

The Moral

_____
_____
_____
_____

The Virtue

_____
_____

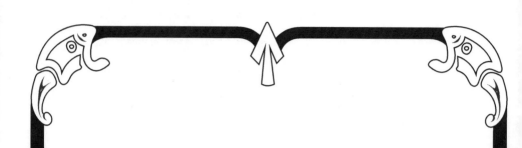

18. Only one who has experienced much and traveled well can have a great amount of wisdom.

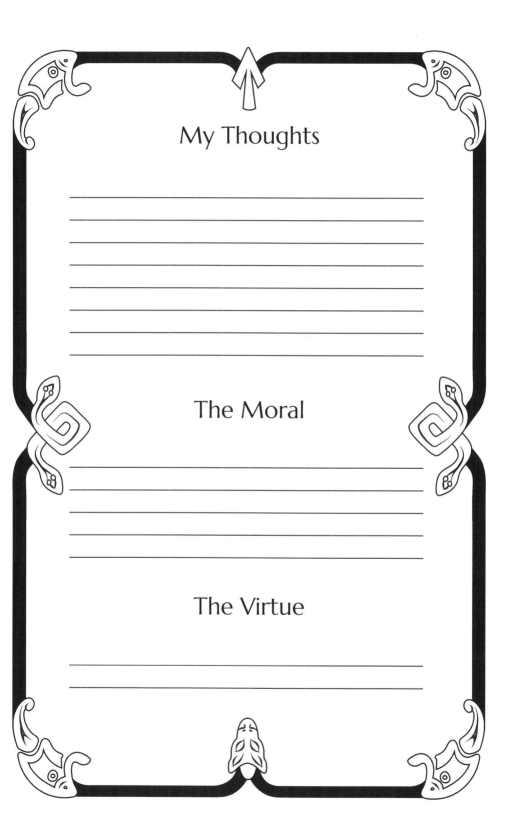

My Thoughts

_____
_____
_____
_____
_____
_____
_____

The Moral

_____
_____
_____
_____

The Virtue

_____
_____

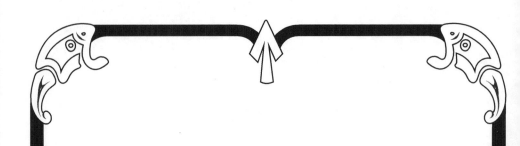

19. One must know how to drink alcohol but drink it moderately.
One must speak sensibly or be silent.
No one will fault you if you must go to bed early.

My Thoughts

_____
_____
_____
_____
_____
_____
_____
_____

The Moral

_____
_____
_____
_____

The Virtue

_____
_____

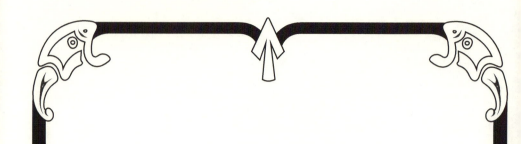

20. Greedy and weak is the one who eats too much and does not use moderation. He will make himself sick because he refuses to use common sense and he will be teased for his fat belly by those wiser than he.

My Thoughts

_____
_____
_____
_____
_____
_____
_____
_____

The Moral

_____
_____
_____
_____
_____

The Virtue

_____
_____

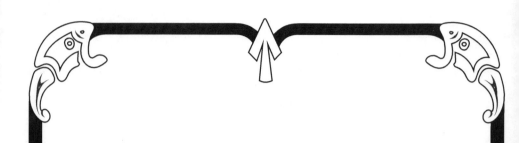

21. Even cows know when it is time to stop eating or they would eat themselves to death.
The weak and foolish man does not stop eating even when he knows he should.

My Thoughts

_____
_____
_____
_____
_____
_____
_____

The Moral

_____
_____
_____
_____

The Virtue

_____
_____

22. A weak and evil person mocks and sneers at everything, but being weak he does not know the one thing he should. That he himself is not free of faults.

My Thoughts

_____
_____
_____
_____
_____
_____
_____

The Moral

_____
_____
_____
_____

The Virtue

_____
_____

23. The fool lays awake at night afraid and worrying.
Thinking about all that causes him distress.
When the morning comes all his worries remain the same but he is also too tired to face the day.

My Thoughts

_____

_____

_____

_____

_____

_____

_____

_____

The Moral

_____

_____

_____

_____

_____

The Virtue

_____

_____

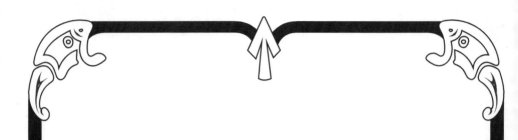

24. A fool thinks that everyone who smiles at them and says nice things to them are their friend and means them no harm.
He does not realize that many of these people hate him, speak poorly of him or seek to harm him.
When he is among the wise, they see what he cannot.

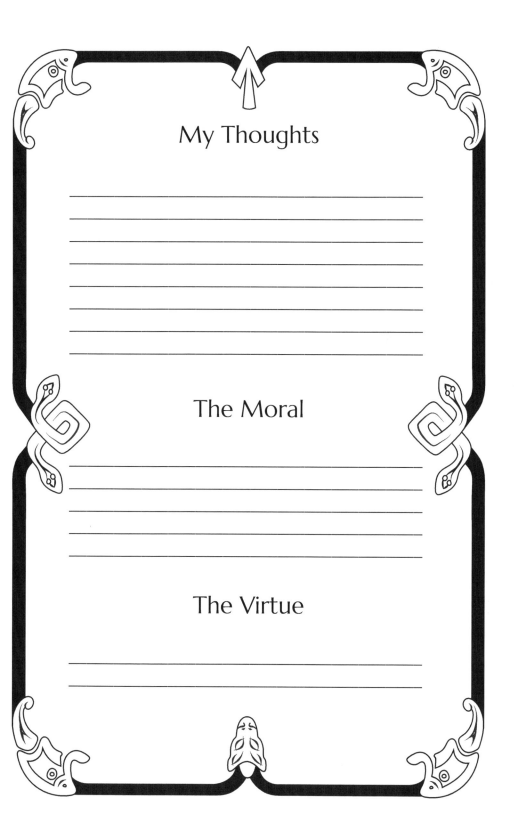

My Thoughts

_____
_____
_____
_____
_____
_____
_____

The Moral

_____
_____
_____
_____
_____

The Virtue

_____
_____

25. A man is unwise who thinks that everyone who is kind to him, is his friend. But he soon learns when in need of help that few will stand beside him as a friend.

My Thoughts

_____
_____
_____
_____
_____
_____
_____

The Moral

_____
_____
_____
_____

The Virtue

_____
_____

26. A Foolish man thinks he knows everything, but when he is asked questions he does not know the answer to any.

My Thoughts

The Moral

The Virtue

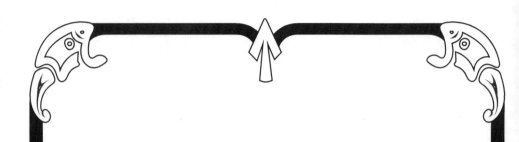

27. When around other people it is best for an unwise man to be quiet.
If he is silent then no one will know that he is unwise, unless he talks too much.
It is better for him to listen and learn from the wise.

My Thoughts

_____
_____
_____
_____
_____
_____
_____

The Moral

_____
_____
_____
_____

The Virtue

_____
_____

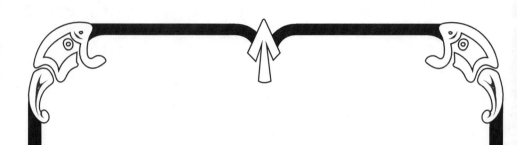

28. Of strong character you seem to others when you know the proper way to ask and answer questions.
If you cannot do this others will know you are not wise.

My Thoughts

_____
_____
_____
_____
_____
_____
_____
_____

The Moral

_____
_____
_____
_____

The Virtue

_____
_____

29. Do not be quick to become angry and speak bad words.
Nor should you talk without a reason.
Do not babble for the sake of hearing yourself speak.
Speaking too much and not holding your tongue when it is necessary will often get you into trouble.

My Thoughts

_____
_____
_____
_____
_____
_____
_____

The Moral

_____
_____
_____
_____
_____

The Virtue

_____
_____

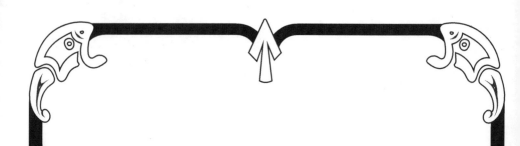

30. An unwise man is better silent when at a gathering.
Others will think him wise enough if he does not show them he is not.

My Thoughts

_____
_____
_____
_____
_____
_____
_____
_____

The Moral

_____
_____
_____
_____
_____

The Virtue

_____
_____

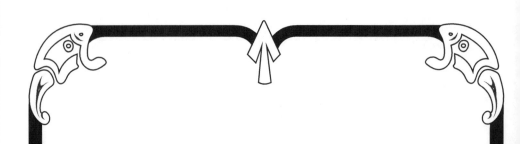

31. Teasing another may make you feel clever but you do not know what enemies you make among the people gathered. Someone who makes fun of others is disliked and thought of as a fool.

My Thoughts

_____
_____
_____
_____
_____
_____
_____
_____

The Moral

_____
_____
_____
_____
_____

The Virtue

_____
_____

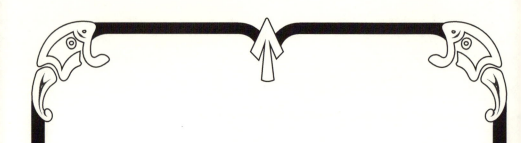

32. Even if we have friends that we like very well.
There will be times when friends disagree and even argue.

My Thoughts

_____
_____
_____
_____
_____
_____
_____

The Moral

_____
_____
_____
_____
_____

The Virtue

_____
_____

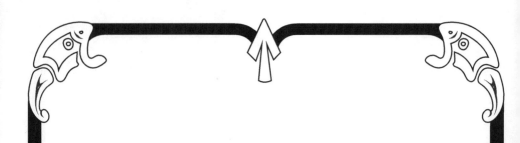

33. Before you go to eat at the home of a friend have a small meal.
You will be a better companion if you are not putting food in your mouth like a wolf the entire visit.

My Thoughts

_____
_____
_____
_____
_____
_____
_____

The Moral

_____
_____
_____
_____

The Virtue

_____
_____

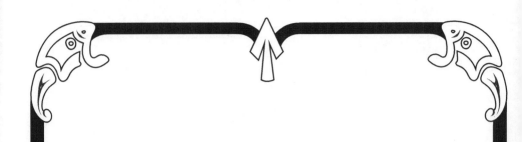

34. Even if a bad friend lives nearby no one wants to visit him.
But with good friends it is joyful and easy to visit them often even if they live further away.

My Thoughts

_____
_____
_____
_____
_____
_____
_____
_____

The Moral

_____
_____
_____
_____
_____

The Virtue

_____
_____

35. Do not take advantage of the people who give you their hospitality.
Even with good friends, if you do not give them their peace, they will no longer enjoy your company.

My Thoughts

_____
_____
_____
_____
_____
_____
_____

The Moral

_____
_____
_____
_____
_____

The Virtue

_____
_____

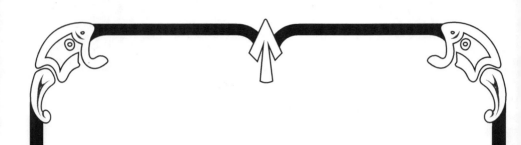

36. One must look after themselves.
It is better to live in a small home than to
beg or take from others.
You are of strong character, the one
who will stand on his own feet and carry
himself as his own responsibility.

My Thoughts

_____

_____

_____

_____

_____

_____

_____

_____

The Moral

_____

_____

_____

_____

The Virtue

_____

_____

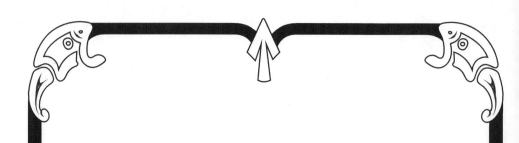

37. One who does not take responsibility for his own care is of a despairing heart.
To live within your ability is better than to ask someone else to feed you every meal.
You are in control in your own home.
When you beg for everything you are no more than a slave.

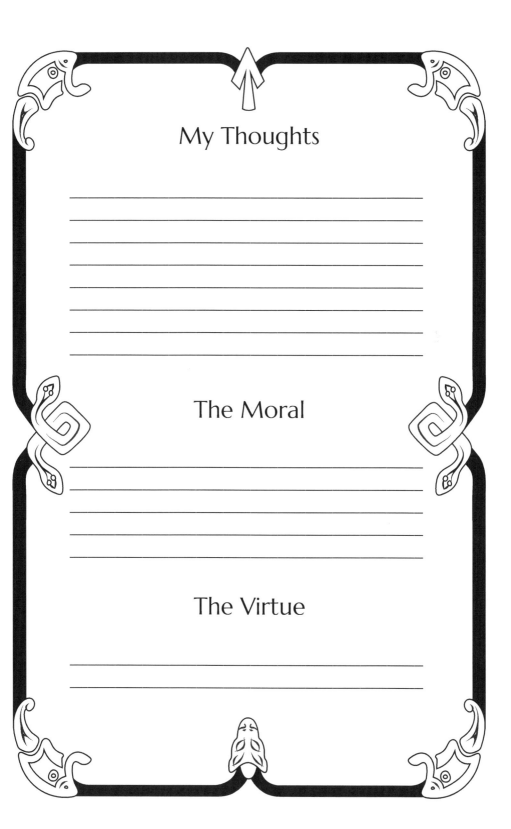

My Thoughts

_____
_____
_____
_____
_____
_____
_____

The Moral

_____
_____
_____
_____

The Virtue

_____
_____

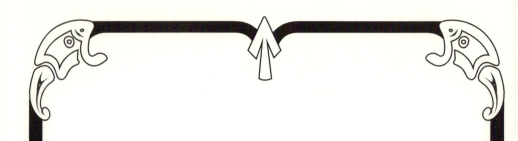

38. Never take one step from home without some means of protecting yourself against harm.
You never know what dangers you may come across when you travel.
No matter how near or far.

My Thoughts

_____
_____
_____
_____
_____
_____
_____
_____

The Moral

_____
_____
_____
_____
_____

The Virtue

_____
_____

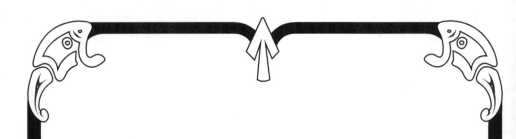

39. Whenever you are given a gift it is best to give a gift of similar kind in return. There has not been a person in this world that was unhappy to receive something kindly given in a gesture of friendship.

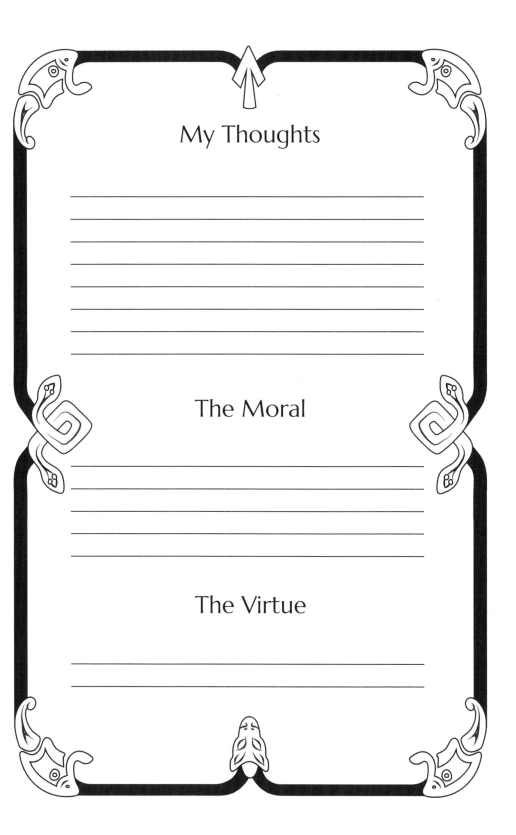

My Thoughts

_____
_____
_____
_____
_____
_____
_____

The Moral

_____
_____
_____
_____

The Virtue

_____
_____

40. Of the money you earn, you should spend it on what you need.
If it is saved to be given to someone you love it is often taken by someone you hate.

My Thoughts

_____
_____
_____
_____
_____
_____
_____

The Moral

_____
_____
_____
_____

The Virtue

_____
_____

41. For a good and lasting friendship it is best to give and receive gifts openly and often.
Joyful we make one another and build our relationship stronger when we show our affections for each other regularly.

My Thoughts

_____
_____
_____
_____
_____
_____
_____
_____

The Moral

_____
_____
_____
_____
_____

The Virtue

_____
_____

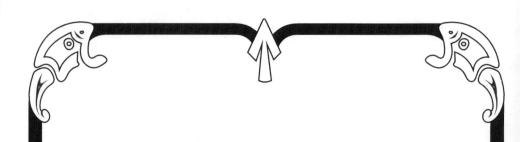

42. To friends give a gift for a gift, laughter for laughter and if lies they give you, repay them with lies.
If a friend lies does that make him a true friend after all?

My Thoughts

_____

_____

_____

_____

_____

_____

_____

The Moral

_____

_____

_____

_____

The Virtue

_____

_____

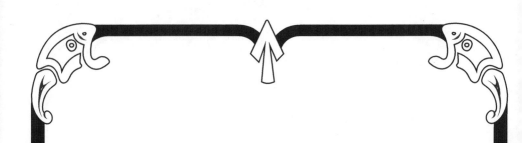

43. To a friend be a friend good and true, but with the friend of your enemy do not make friends because you will never know where their loyalties will lie.

My Thoughts

_____
_____
_____
_____
_____
_____
_____
_____

The Moral

_____
_____
_____
_____

The Virtue

_____
_____

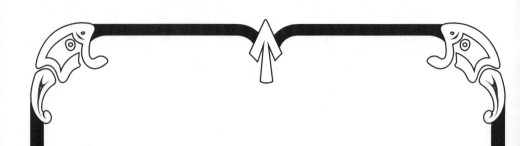

44. If you have a friend who you love dearly and who you truly trust.
If you would want a good relationship with them to continue, go to see them often, speak your thoughts and dreams to them, and exchange gifts.

My Thoughts

_____
_____
_____
_____
_____
_____
_____

The Moral

_____
_____
_____
_____

The Virtue

_____
_____

45. In regards to a friend who you do not trust but do not want to have any trouble from.
Say kind things but do not share your mind with them.
If they lie to you give them lies in return.

My Thoughts

_____
_____
_____
_____
_____
_____
_____
_____
_____

The Moral

_____
_____
_____
_____
_____

The Virtue

_____
_____
_____

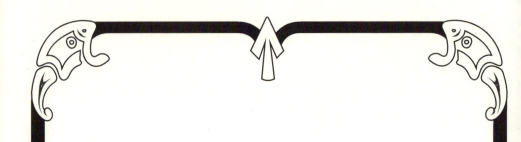

46. Again it is important to emphasis, people who you do not trust and who's thoughts you doubt to be truthful.
Use common sense and cunning when dealing with them.
Laugh with them but do not share your true thoughts.
Remember a gift for a gift must be repaid.

My Thoughts

_____
_____
_____
_____
_____
_____
_____

The Moral

_____
_____
_____
_____

The Virtue

_____
_____

47. When I was young, I traveled alone and became lost.
When I made a friend, I was no longer alone and my heart was filled with joy.
Companionship is better than isolation.

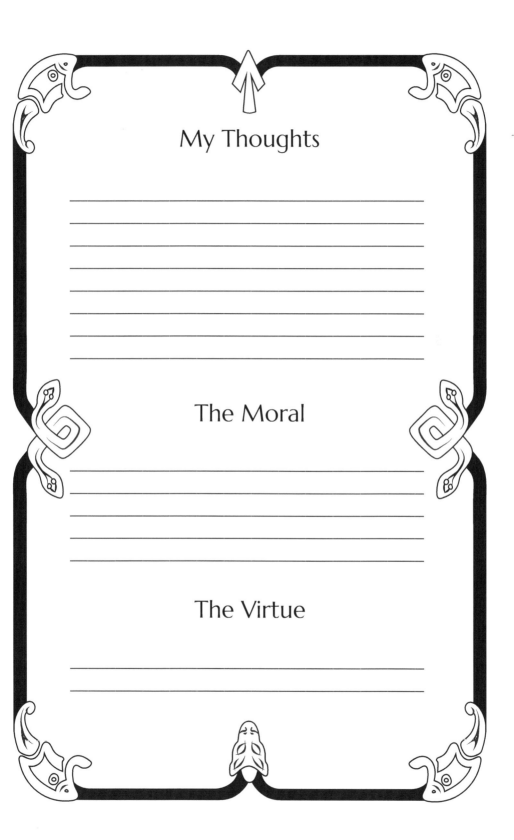

My Thoughts

_____
_____
_____
_____
_____
_____
_____

The Moral

_____
_____
_____
_____

The Virtue

_____
_____

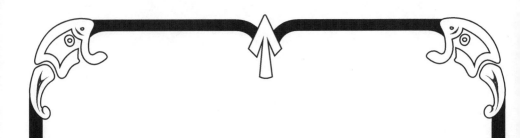

48. The best life is that of one who is noble, generous and brave.
They do not spend their time in sadness or worry.
But a weak minded person is afraid of everything.
They are miserable, selfish and greedy.

My Thoughts

_____
_____
_____
_____
_____
_____
_____
_____

The Moral

_____
_____
_____
_____

The Virtue

_____
_____

49. If you see someone who is need of help that you can provide, offer them a hand.
Often you can help someone in trouble restore their dignity.

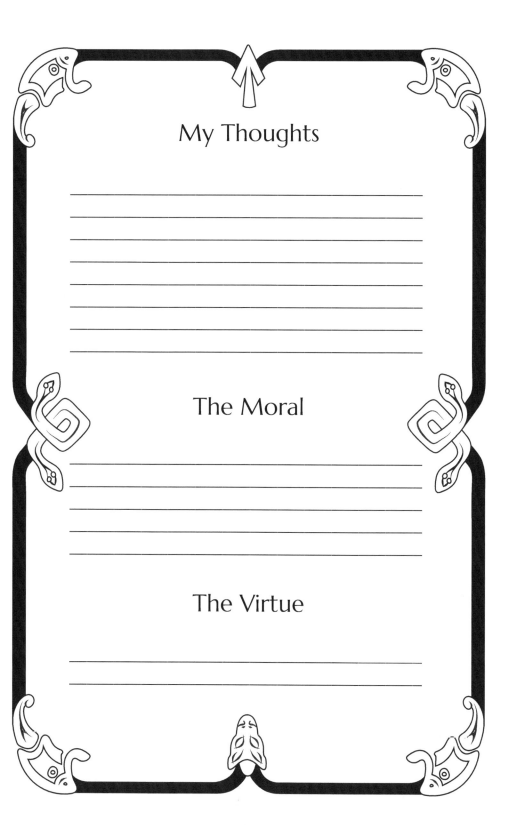

My Thoughts

_____
_____
_____
_____
_____
_____
_____

The Moral

_____
_____
_____
_____

The Virtue

_____
_____

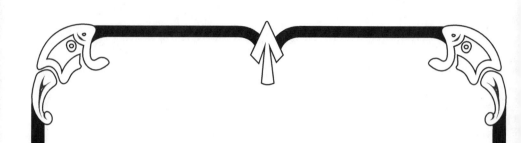

50. What is life without love?
Love* is what makes life worth living.

Love: Does not only mean the love of a partner, but the
love of your family, your children and your friends.

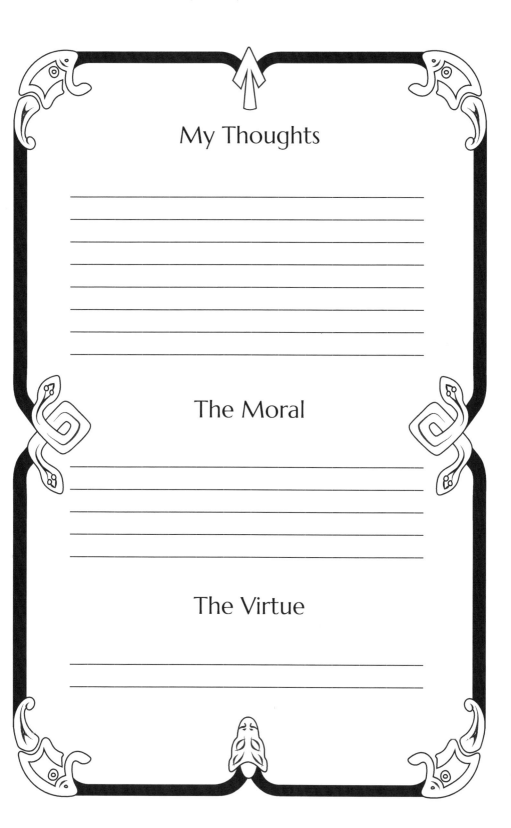

My Thoughts

_____
_____
_____
_____
_____
_____
_____
_____

The Moral

_____
_____
_____
_____
_____

The Virtue

_____
_____

51. You may think a new friendship will be strong because you seem to have the same sort of passion but quickly that friendship turns bad when the same excited passion turns to strong dislike.

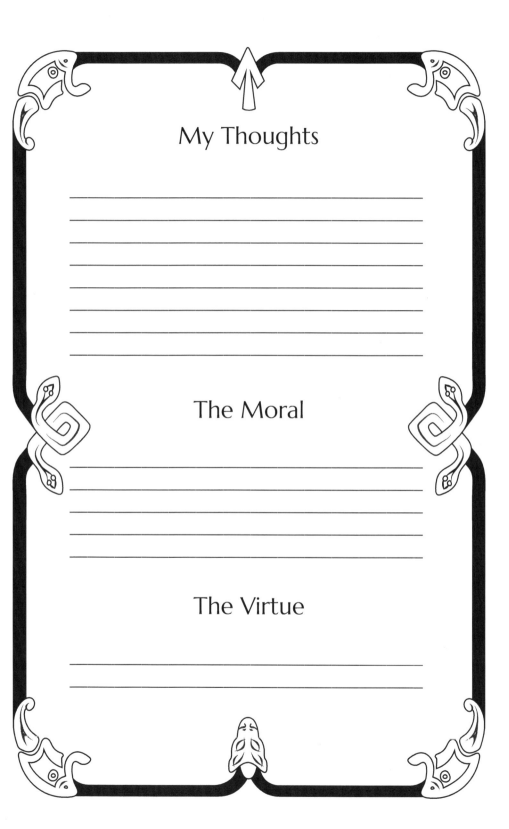

My Thoughts

The Moral

The Virtue

52. To earn a good and strong friendship you do not need to give much.
Even a piece of food or a drink will be enough to earn you a good friend.

My Thoughts

The Moral

The Virtue

53. Not all people in the world are wise and none are equally wise.
But one thing everyone has in common is that we all have at least some common sense.

My Thoughts

_____
_____
_____
_____
_____
_____
_____
_____

The Moral

_____
_____
_____
_____
_____

The Virtue

_____
_____

54. Like all things call for moderation, one should have a good amount of common sense but not spend all of their time seeking ever more wisdom.
The happiest people are those who know a lot but don't over concern themselves with trying to know everything.

My Thoughts

The Moral

The Virtue

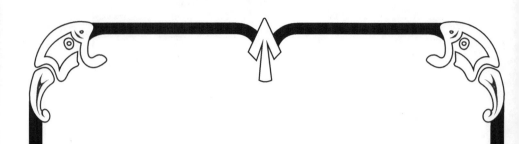

55. It is important to have a good amount of wisdom but to know too much is to never find happiness.
Remember happiness is necessary for a life well lived.

My Thoughts

_____
_____
_____
_____
_____
_____
_____
_____

The Moral

_____
_____
_____
_____
_____

The Virtue

_____
_____

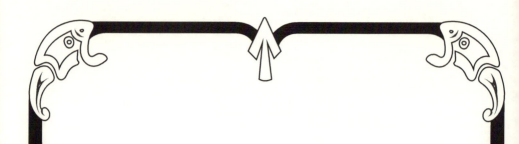

56. Do not seek to know more than you should.
No one should know what their future is until it is upon them.
Knowing your fate will only cause you sadness.

My Thoughts

_____
_____
_____
_____
_____
_____
_____

The Moral

_____
_____
_____
_____

The Virtue

_____
_____

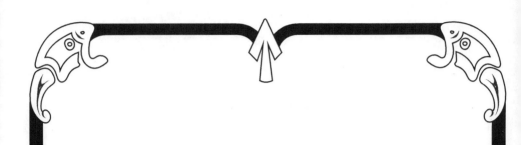

57. You will grow in praise from others by the use of good speech.
The foolish who do not know how to speak will not be remembered.

My Thoughts

_____
_____
_____
_____
_____
_____
_____
_____

The Moral

_____
_____
_____
_____

The Virtue

_____
_____

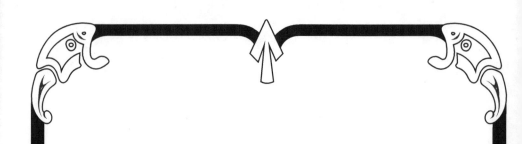

58. To be successful you must get up early.
If you sleep in you waste valuable time.
Don't be lazy.
The lazy accomplish little.

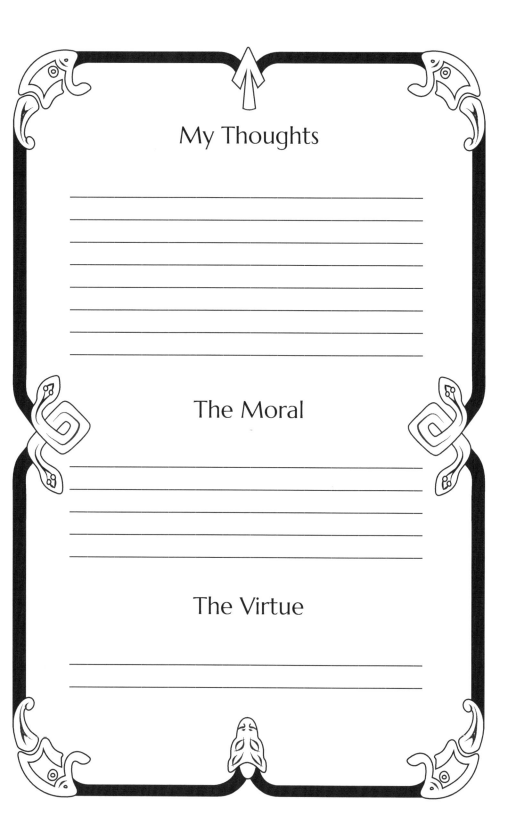

My Thoughts

_____
_____
_____
_____
_____
_____
_____
_____

The Moral

_____
_____
_____
_____

The Virtue

_____
_____

59. Get up early if you have much to do. If you don't get up early you wont finish what you need to.
How much money you earn depends on how much you apply yourself to your work.

My Thoughts

_____
_____
_____
_____
_____
_____
_____
_____

The Moral

_____
_____
_____
_____
_____

The Virtue

_____
_____

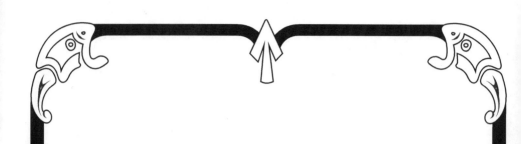

60. It is important to be prepared for all that may come in the future.
You must have wisdom to understand what you will need for the future.

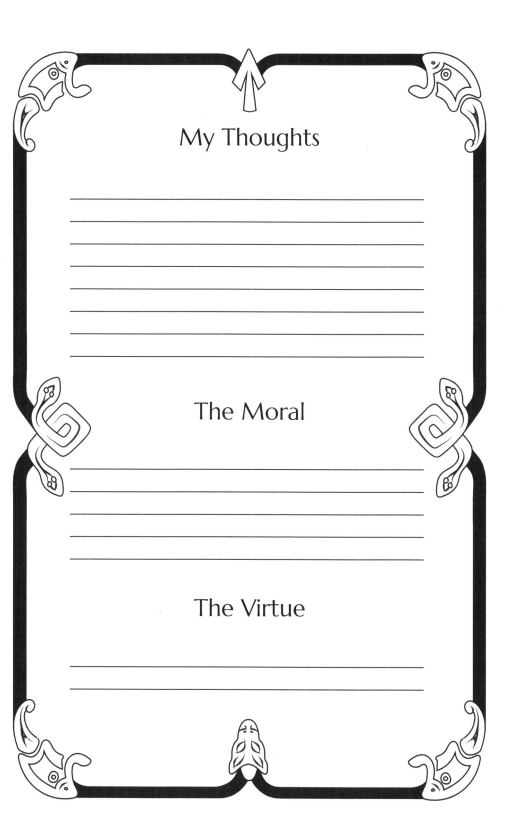

My Thoughts

_____
_____
_____
_____
_____
_____
_____
_____

The Moral

_____
_____
_____
_____
_____

The Virtue

_____
_____

61. Never be ashamed if you do not have the newest or the nicest clothing. Rather what is important is to always be clean, presentable and have a full belly when you go to a gathering.

My Thoughts

_____
_____
_____
_____
_____
_____
_____
_____

The Moral

_____
_____
_____
_____

The Virtue

_____
_____

62. Shocked and surprised is the unwise when he finds among many people no one will speak in his defense.

My Thoughts

_____
_____
_____
_____
_____
_____
_____

The Moral

_____
_____
_____
_____

The Virtue

_____
_____

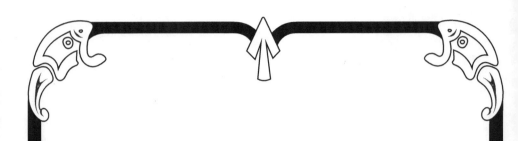

63. If you want to be thought of as wise by others you must know how to think before you speak and you must know how to ask and answer correctly.

If you have a secret that you must share, let one person know who you trust, but no more than one.

If three people know your secret it will be known to everyone.

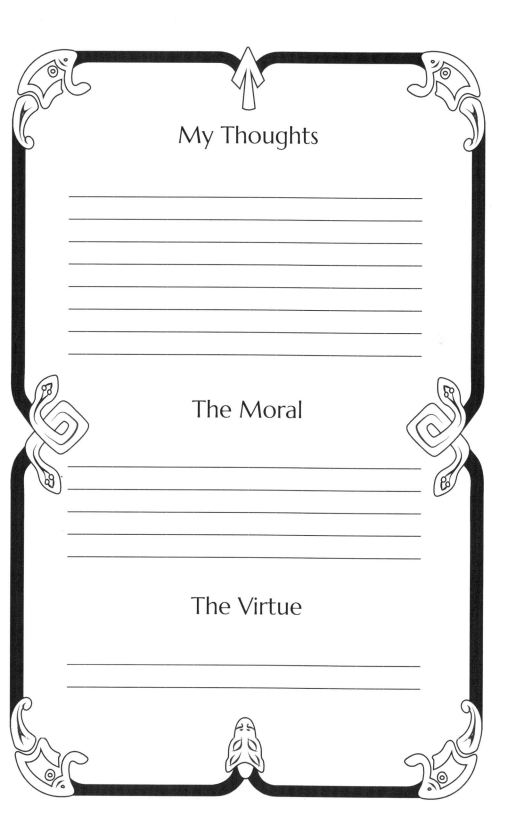

My Thoughts

_____
_____
_____
_____
_____
_____
_____

The Moral

_____
_____
_____
_____

The Virtue

_____
_____

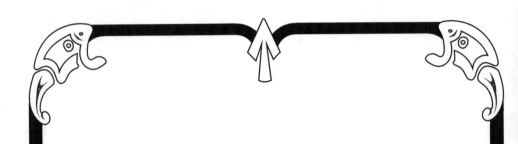

64. The wise must always remember that when he comes among others to be careful and measured.
He must remember even though he may be powerful, he is not the most powerful. And though he is wise he is not the wisest of all.

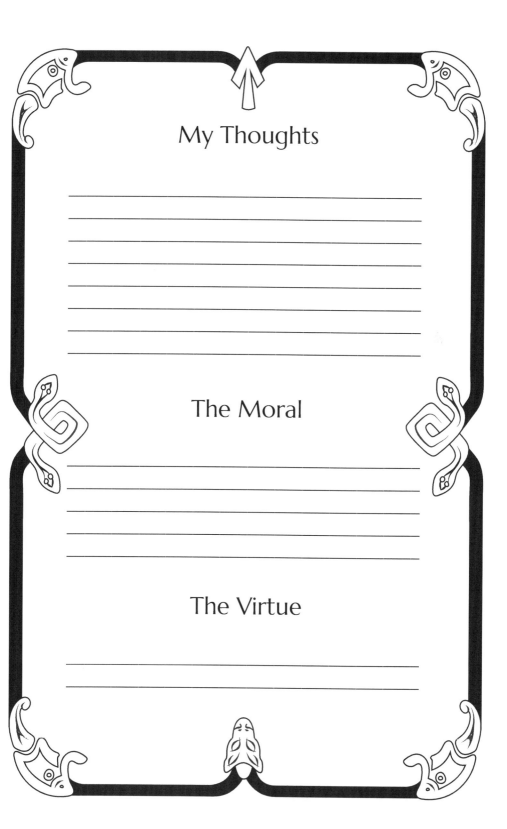

My Thoughts

_____
_____
_____
_____
_____
_____
_____
_____

The Moral

_____
_____
_____
_____

The Virtue

_____
_____

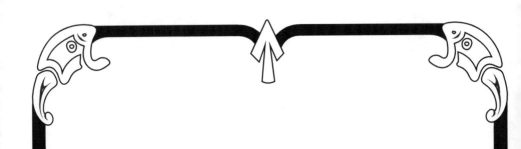

65. Be careful of what you say to others, even if they are your friends.
The things you share with others often end up being used against you.

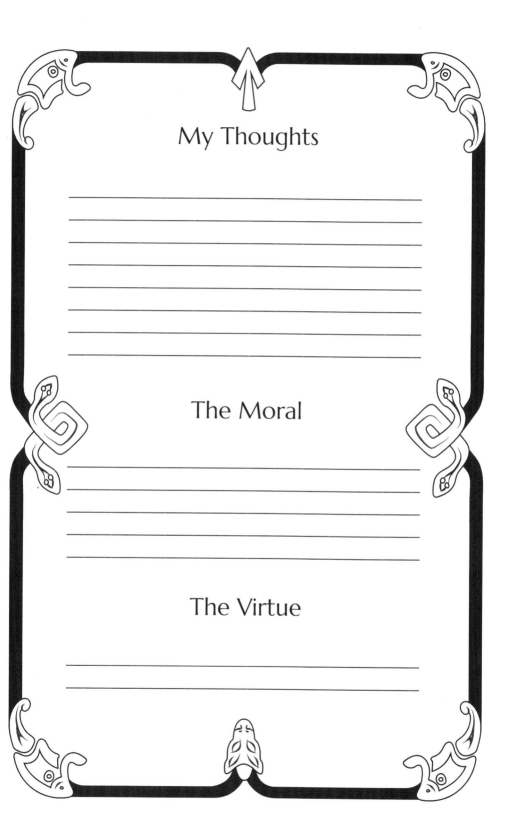

My Thoughts

_____
_____
_____
_____
_____
_____
_____

The Moral

_____
_____
_____
_____

The Virtue

_____
_____

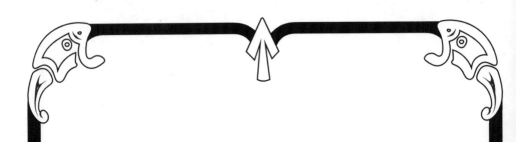

66. The foolish man rarely knows when the time is right or wrong for going to visit others.
Pay attention to the way people react to you and chose the right timing wisely.
If you do not then you will find many people dislike you.

My Thoughts

_____
_____
_____
_____
_____
_____
_____
_____

The Moral

_____
_____
_____
_____
_____

The Virtue

_____
_____

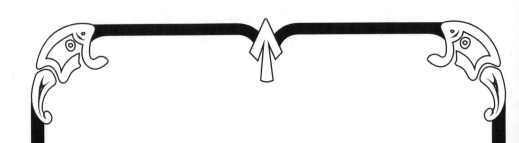

67. Always remember to be hospitable. If you invite a guest to your home offer them plenty of food and refreshments. Make them feel comfortable and well regarded.

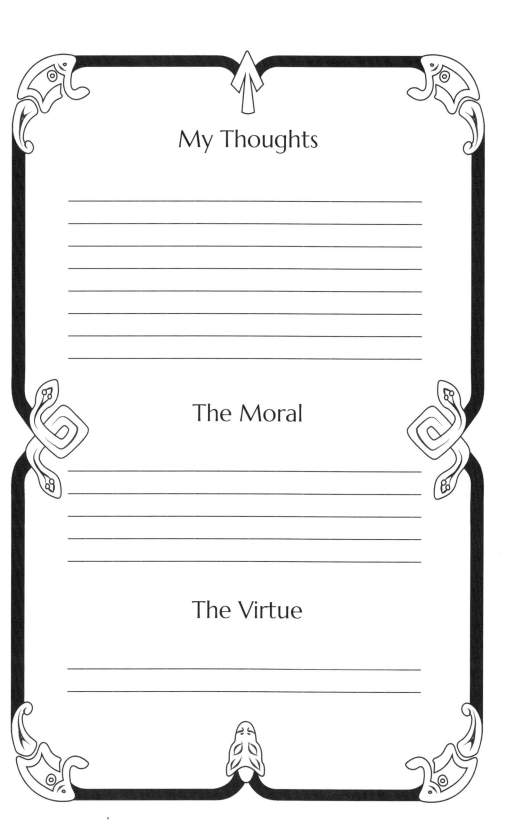

My Thoughts

_____
_____
_____
_____
_____
_____
_____

The Moral

_____
_____
_____
_____

The Virtue

_____
_____

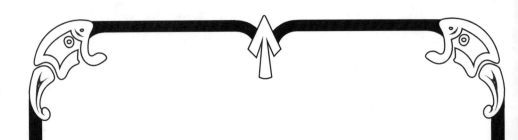

68. Remember that you should never despair.
Even in our darkest moments there are things to find joy in.
The sight of the sun is one.
Good health is another.
To live our lives without shame is the best of all.

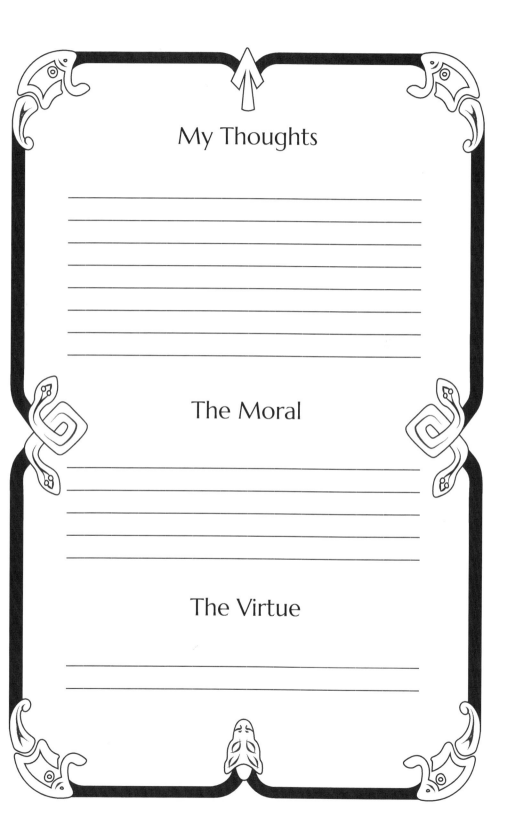

My Thoughts

_____
_____
_____
_____
_____
_____
_____

The Moral

_____
_____
_____
_____

The Virtue

_____
_____

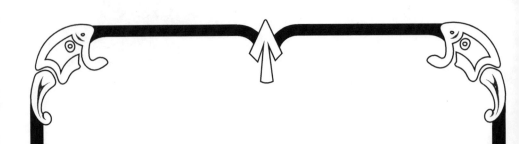

69. Not everything is bad even if you are terribly ill.
You can find happiness in your children, or the life you have built, the money you have or the work you do.

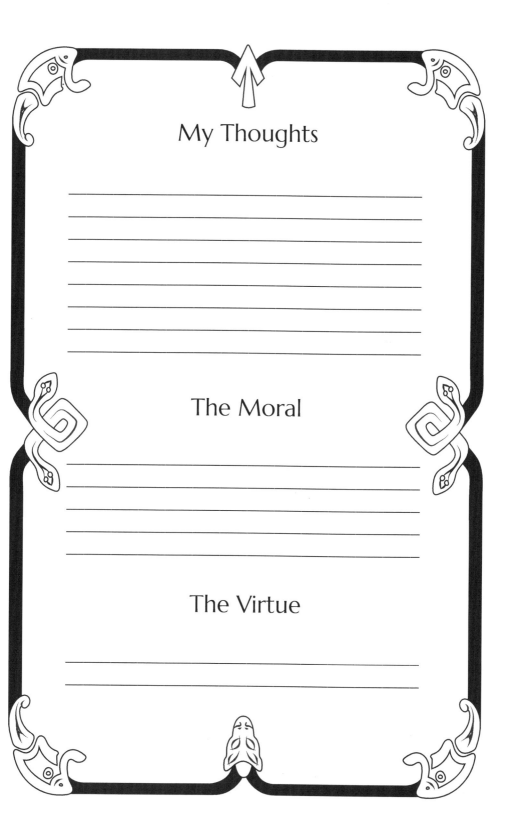

My Thoughts

_____
_____
_____
_____
_____
_____
_____

The Moral

_____
_____
_____
_____

The Virtue

_____
_____

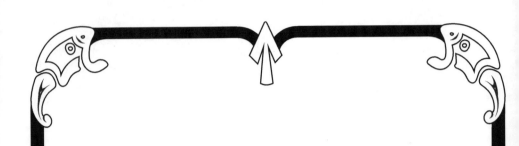

70. It is always better to be alive than dead, even if you are poor or in crisis. If you are alive, your life can always be improved.

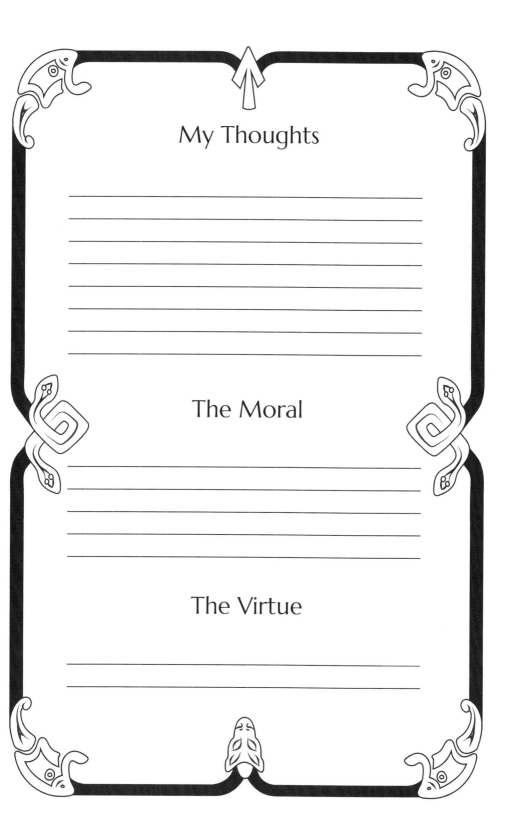

My Thoughts

_____
_____
_____
_____
_____
_____
_____
_____

The Moral

_____
_____
_____
_____

The Virtue

_____
_____

71. It is better to be alive than to be dead, even if you are handicapped in some way. There is always something you can do even if you are different from other people.
Be resourceful.
Remember there is always a reason to live.

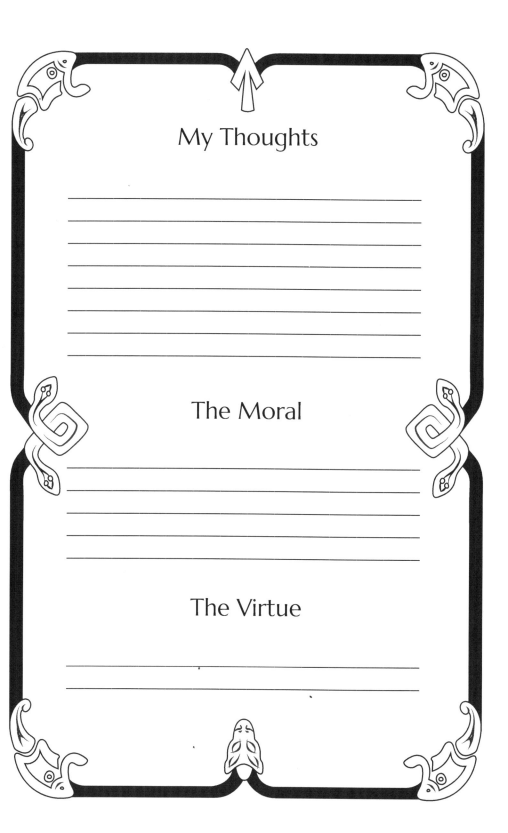

My Thoughts

_____
_____
_____
_____
_____
_____
_____
_____

The Moral

_____
_____
_____
_____
_____

The Virtue

_____
_____

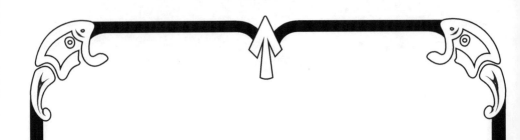

72. Most important than all else is to have children.
Even if your children are born after you have since died.
Rarely are you remembered by anyone other than your family.

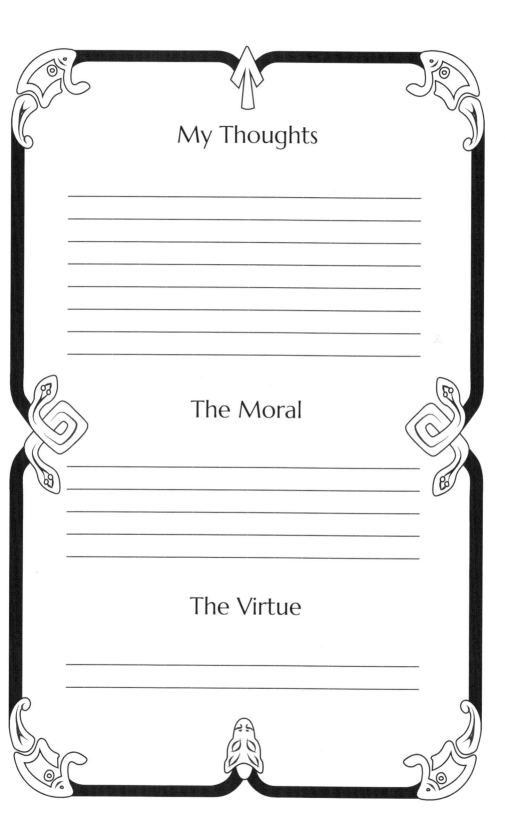

My Thoughts

_____
_____
_____
_____
_____
_____
_____
_____

The Moral

_____
_____
_____
_____

The Virtue

_____
_____

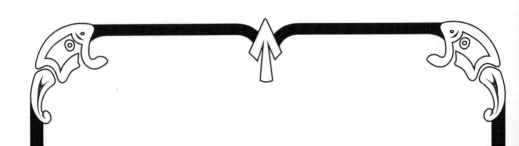

73. Do not be so quick to start a fight or respond to an enemy with sharp words. Always be watchful that someone may be looking for a fight with you.

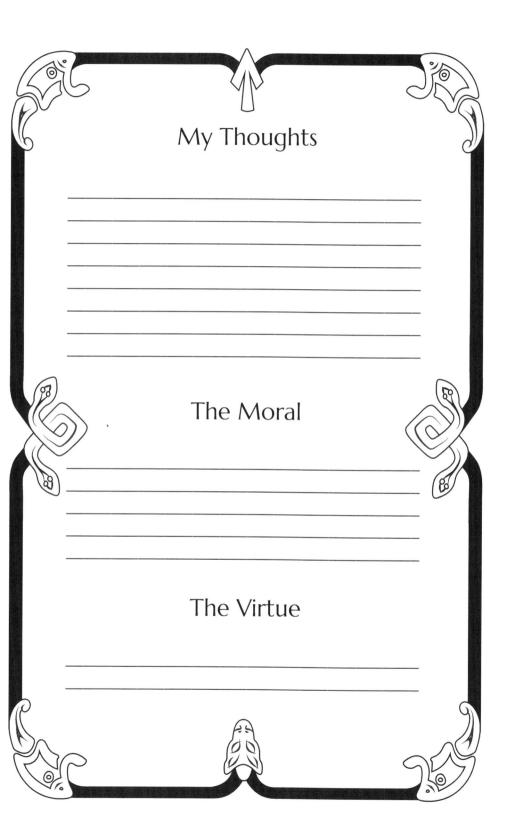

My Thoughts

_____
_____
_____
_____
_____
_____
_____

The Moral

_____
_____
_____
_____

The Virtue

_____
_____

74. If you are well prepared for what may come then you have nothing to fear. The darkness and cold of night cannot harm you, nor the changing of the weather.

My Thoughts

_____
_____
_____
_____
_____
_____
_____

The Moral

_____
_____
_____
_____

The Virtue

_____
_____

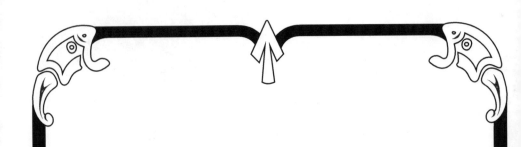

75. Do not tease or make a fool of others. Some people are rich and others are poor. None should be blamed or teased for their life situation.

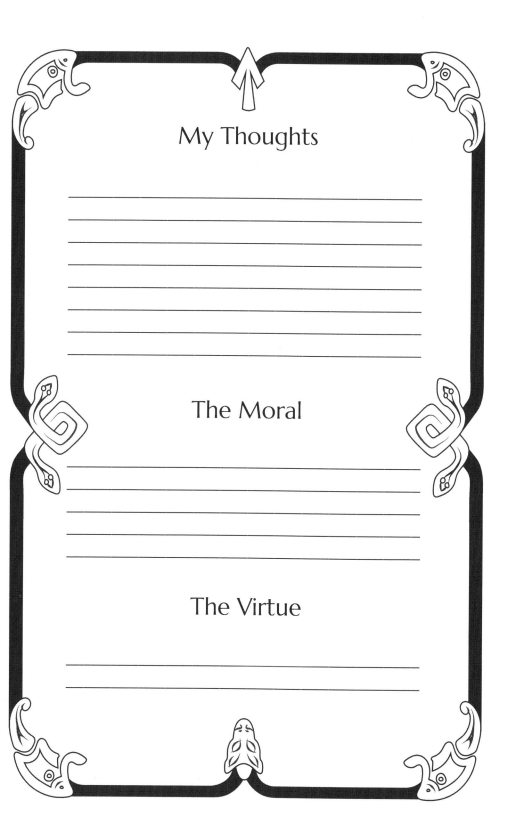

My Thoughts

_____
_____
_____
_____
_____
_____
_____

The Moral

_____
_____
_____
_____

The Virtue

_____
_____

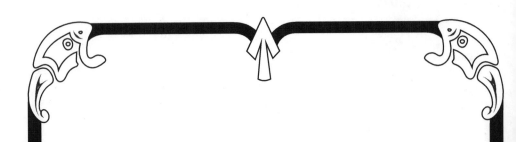

76. All living things die and you will die one day too.
But the one thing that never dies is the good fame you earn for yourself through your good deeds.
Live a life striving for excellence and you will be remembered well.

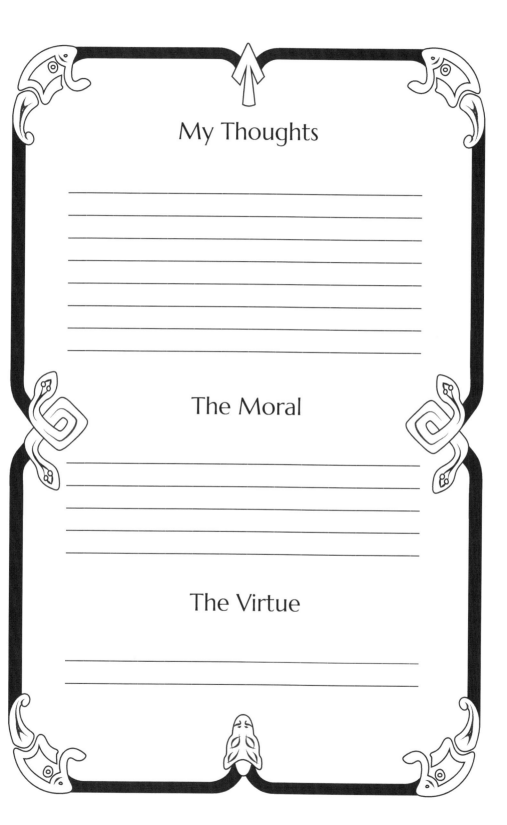

My Thoughts

_____
_____
_____
_____
_____
_____
_____
_____

The Moral

_____
_____
_____
_____

The Virtue

_____
_____

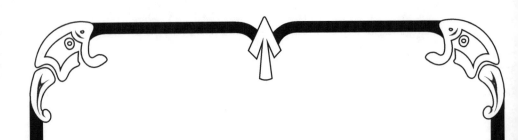

77. All living things die and you will die one day too.
But one thing that never dies is how you will be judged after your life is done.
Live a life of weakness and you will be remembered as a fool.

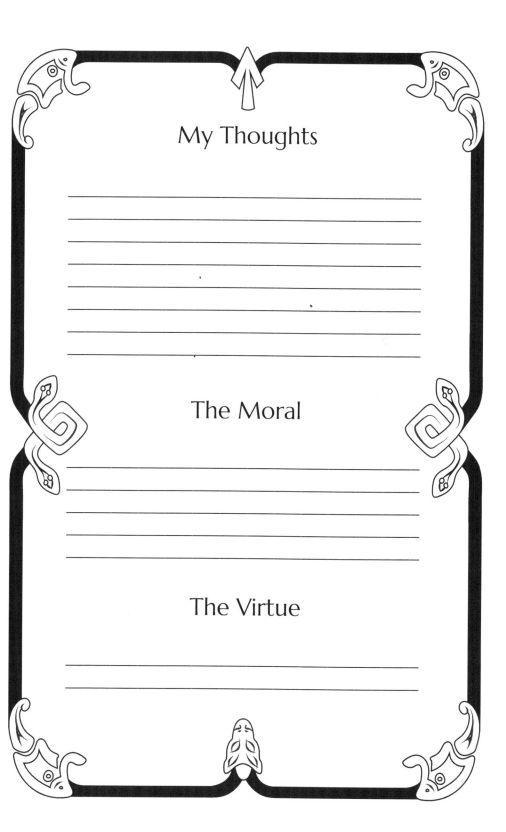

My Thoughts

_____
_____
_____
_____
_____
_____
_____
_____

The Moral

_____
_____
_____
_____
_____

The Virtue

_____
_____

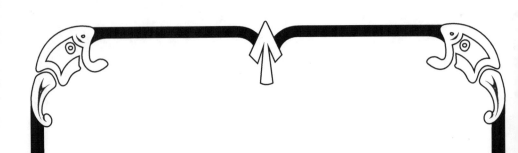

78. Never trust in the money you gain. Wealth is not constant and can be gone in the blink of an eye.

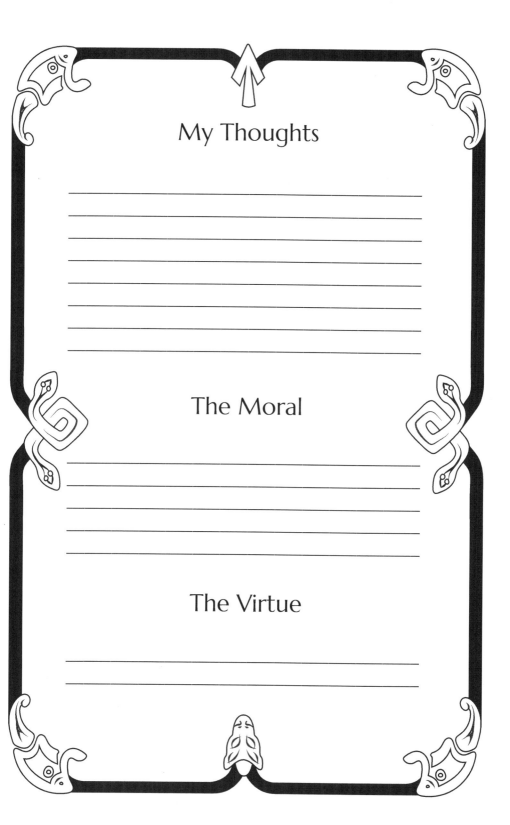

My Thoughts

_____
_____
_____
_____
_____
_____
_____
_____

The Moral

_____
_____
_____
_____

The Virtue

_____
_____

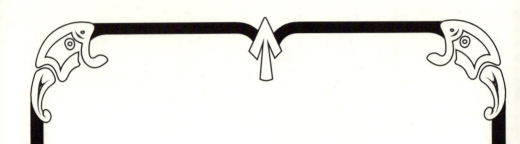

79. A lucky fool may gain wealth and love but he does not gain in wisdom.
With these gifts rather his arrogance and pride grows.
He soon may find he loses all he has gained because of his lack of wisdom.

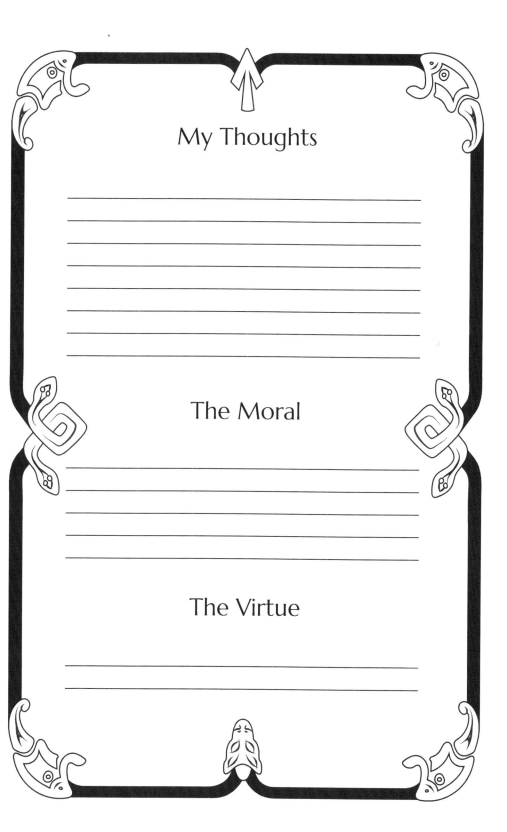

My Thoughts

_____
_____
_____
_____
_____
_____
_____

The Moral

_____
_____
_____
_____

The Virtue

_____
_____

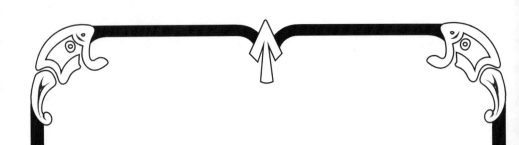

80. From the Runes, if asked a question, the truth will be told. It is then best to keep it quiet.

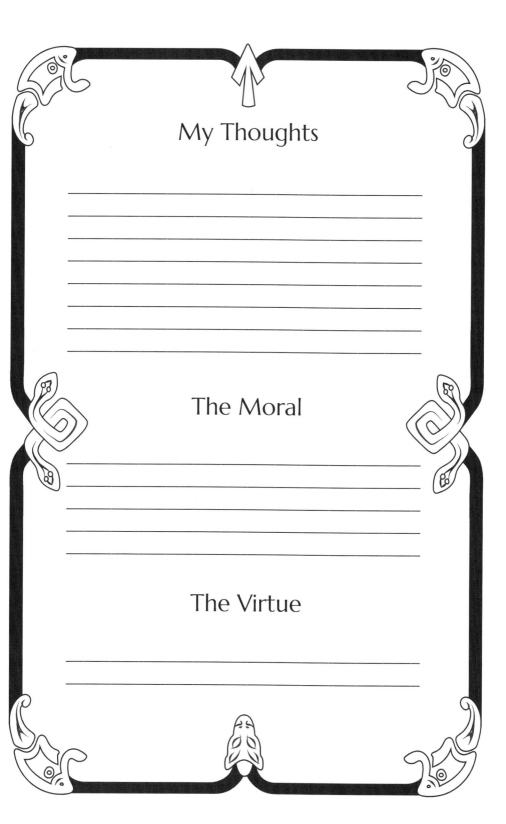

My Thoughts

_____
_____
_____
_____
_____
_____
_____

The Moral

_____
_____
_____
_____

The Virtue

_____
_____

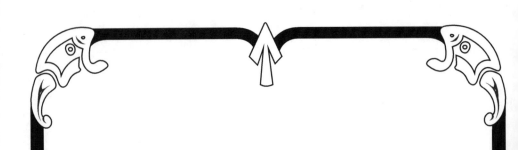

81. Do not give anything praise before it is fully proven to deserve it.

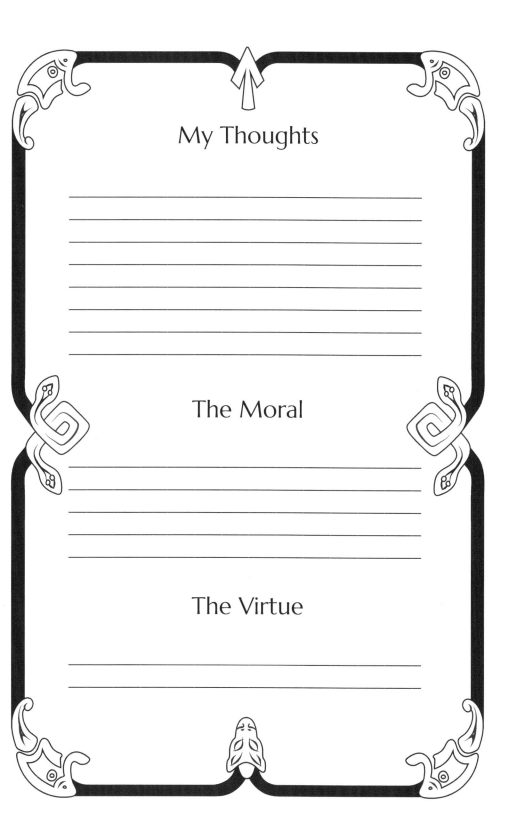

My Thoughts

_____
_____
_____
_____
_____
_____
_____

The Moral

_____
_____
_____
_____

The Virtue

_____
_____

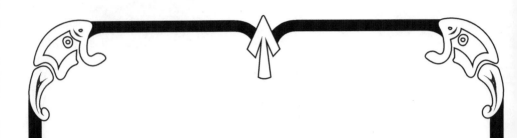

82. Practical Advice:
Cut wood in the wind.
Sail to sea on a breeze.
Talk with a love interest in the privacy of night.
Have a ship that is good at sailing.
Have a sturdy shield for protection.
Have a strong sword for striking.
Have a fair woman for a tender kiss.

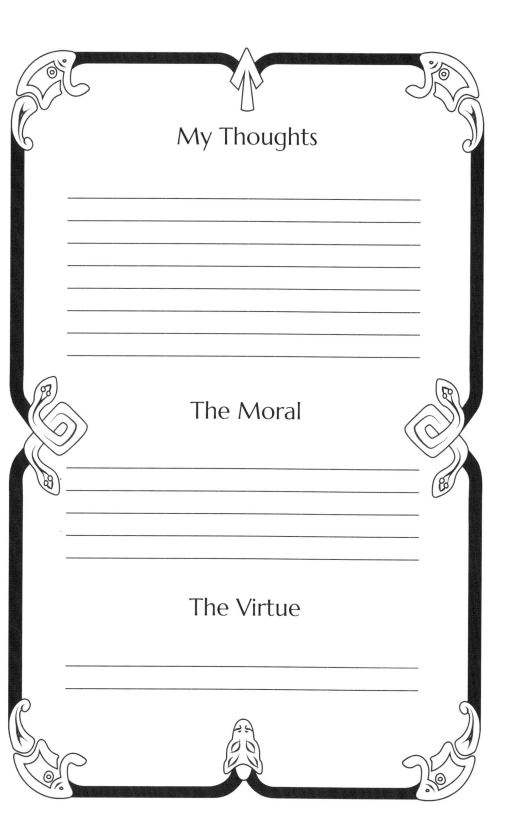

My Thoughts

_____
_____
_____
_____
_____
_____
_____
_____

The Moral

_____
_____
_____
_____
_____

The Virtue

_____
_____

83. More Practical Advice:
Drink beer by the fire.
Use skates to cross ice.
Buy a thin horse.
Buy a rusted Sword.
Feed your horse in a stable.
Feed your dog in your home.

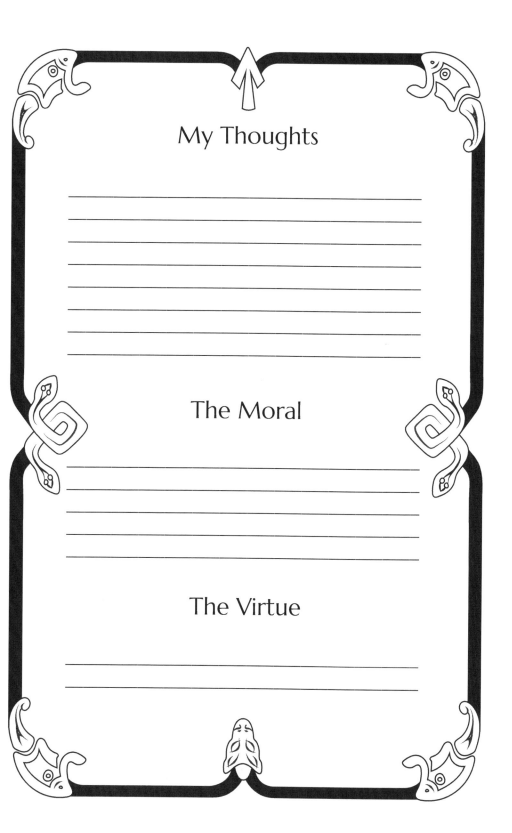

My Thoughts

_____
_____
_____
_____
_____
_____
_____
_____

The Moral

_____
_____
_____
_____

The Virtue

_____
_____

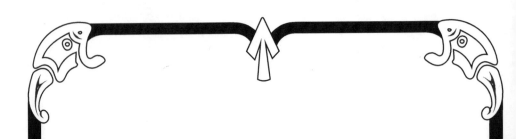

84. Advice to Young Men: Be wary to trust
in the words of a young woman nor trust
any oath she makes.
In their youth their hearts and thoughts
are easily changed.
Deceit is often the result.

*Advice to Young Women: Be true to
yourself and your ancestors. Do not let
your mind easily be swayed by emotions.
There are many evil people who would try
to change your mind by appealing to your
heart.

* The advice to young women is not from the original
poem however it is worth noting that young women are
not always as the stanza says.
If a woman uses her common sense she will not be easily
controlled by emotions. Young men are capable of being
swayed by emotions as well. It is something we all must
be careful to avoid.

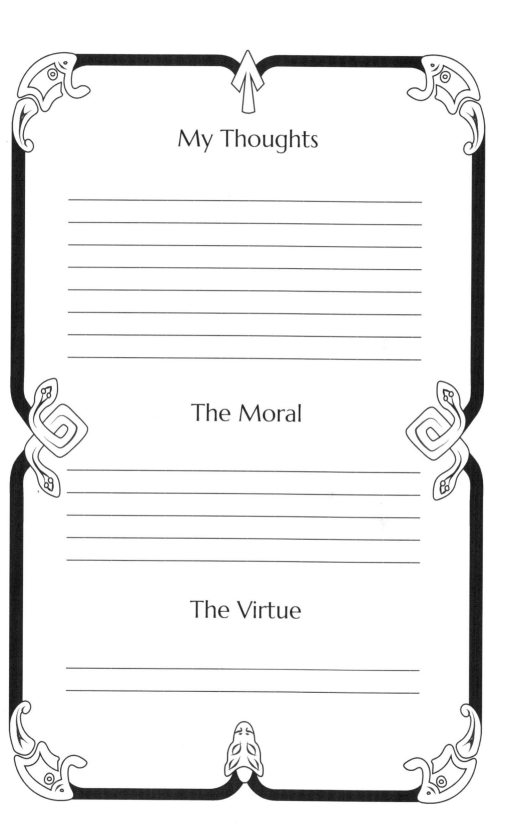

My Thoughts

_____
_____
_____
_____
_____
_____
_____
_____

The Moral

_____
_____
_____
_____

The Virtue

_____
_____

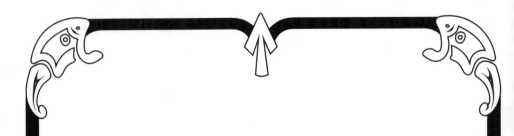

85. Practical Advice - Things you should not trust:
A breaking bow.
A flaring flame.
A greedy wolf.
A croaking raven.
A rooting pig.
A tree with broken roots.
A swelling wave.
A boiling kettle.

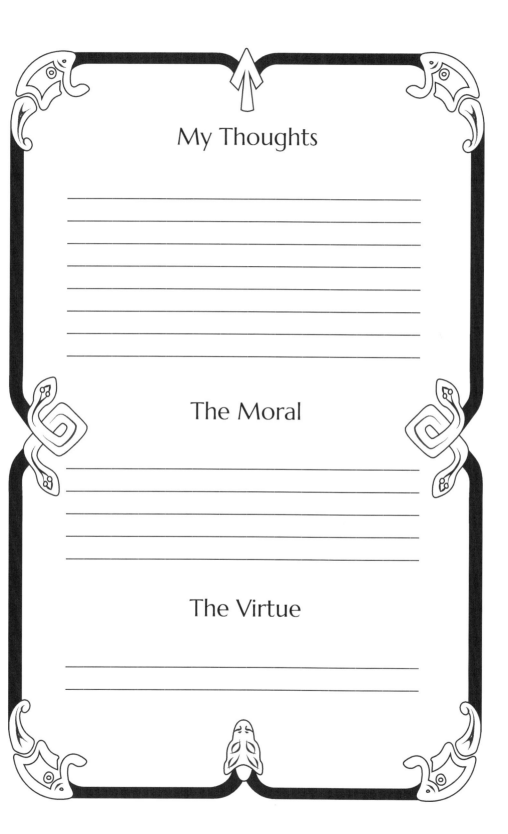

My Thoughts

_____
_____
_____
_____
_____
_____
_____
_____

The Moral

_____
_____
_____
_____
_____

The Virtue

_____
_____

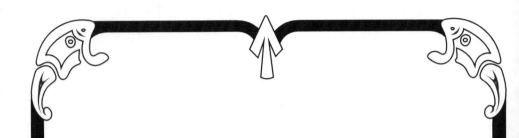

86. More things you should not trust:
Flying arrows.
Receding water.
Newly formed ice.
A coiled snake.
What a woman says in bed.
A broken sword.
The sport of bears.
A royal child.

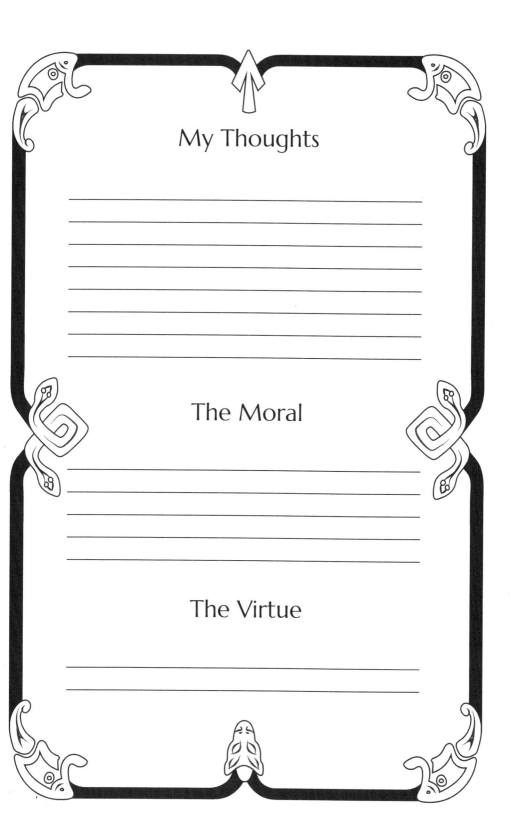

My Thoughts

_____
_____
_____
_____
_____
_____

The Moral

_____
_____
_____
_____

The Virtue

_____
_____

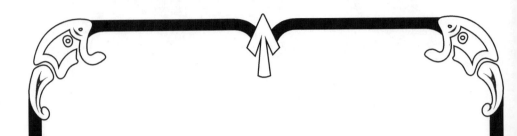

87. More things you should not trust:
A sickly calf.
A slave by choice.
A flattering prophetess.
A freshly killed foe.
A calm sky.
A laughing host.
A barking dog. A grieving harlot.*

*Harlot is a word for a woman who has no morals, a prostitute. Discuss this concept with your parents. How were Harlots regarded by our ancestors?

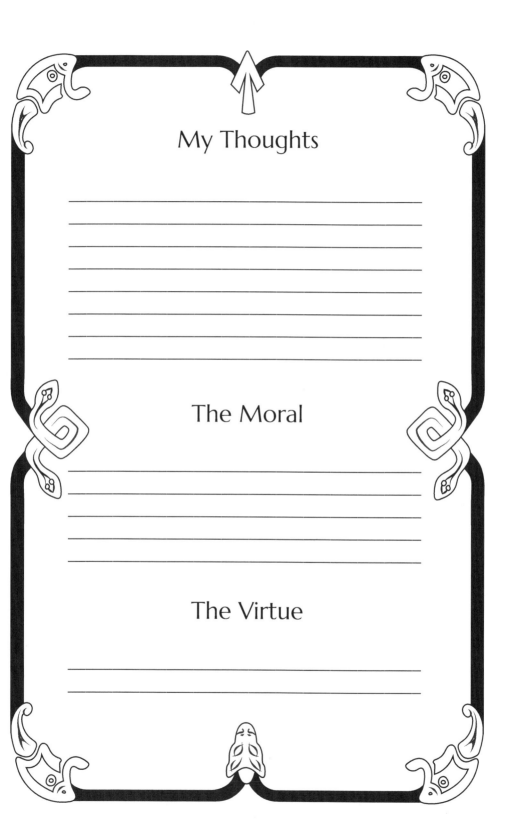

My Thoughts

_____
_____
_____
_____
_____
_____
_____
_____

The Moral

_____
_____
_____
_____

The Virtue

_____
_____

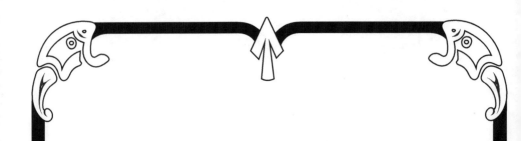

88. More things you should not trust:
A field that has just been planted. It could easily fail.
A child, they do not yet have wisdom, whim* rules their minds.
Don't put your faith into something before it comes to fruition.

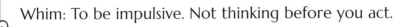
Whim: To be impulsive. Not thinking before you act.

My Thoughts

_____
_____
_____
_____
_____
_____
_____
_____

The Moral

_____
_____
_____
_____
_____

The Virtue

_____
_____

89. More things you should not trust:
A kinslayer*.
A half-burned house.
A horse that is too fast (the horse is useless if a leg is broken).
No one should trust in any of these things.

* Kinslayer means someone who kills a member of their family. Discuss this concept with your parents. Why is it considered worse than murdering someone who is not family? What did our ancestors do to kinslayers?

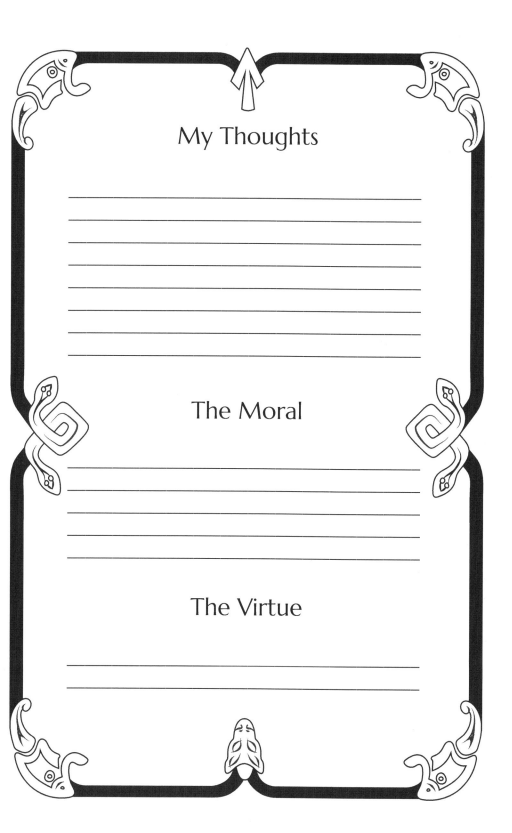

My Thoughts

_____
_____
_____
_____
_____
_____
_____
_____

The Moral

_____
_____
_____
_____
_____

The Virtue

_____
_____

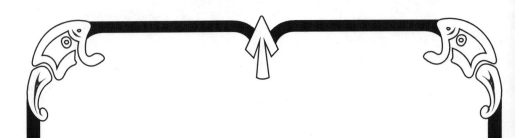

90. More things you should not trust:
The love of a woman whose thoughts are lies.
An untamed horse.
Steering a rudderless ship in a storm.
A hurt leg to hunt for food on slippery terrain.

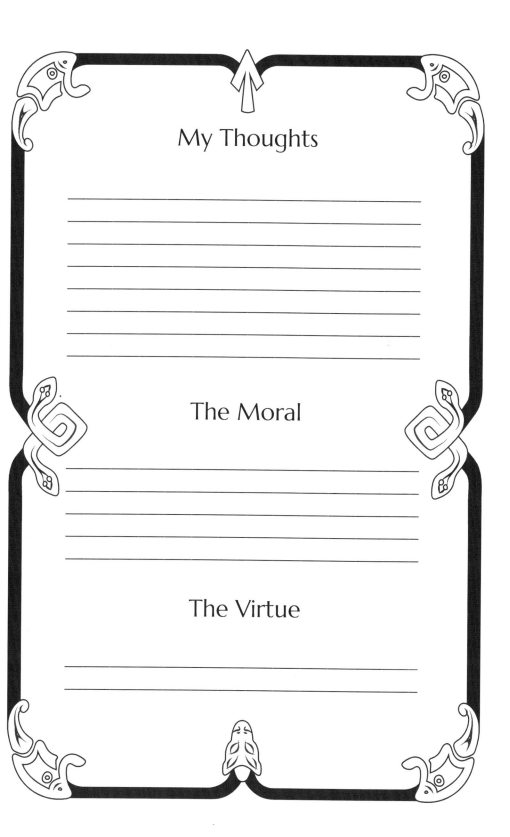

My Thoughts

_____
_____
_____
_____
_____
_____
_____

The Moral

_____
_____
_____
_____

The Virtue

_____
_____

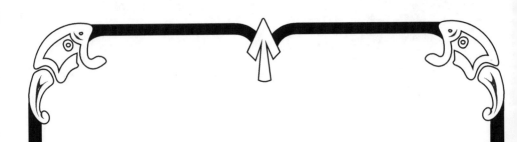

91. Because I know the minds of both men and women, I will speak plainly.
Men are often untruthful to women.
Men will speak most fair when their thoughts are most false.
Even the wisest woman can be swayed by their lies.
To Young Women: When a man flatters you and promises you things be very cautious.

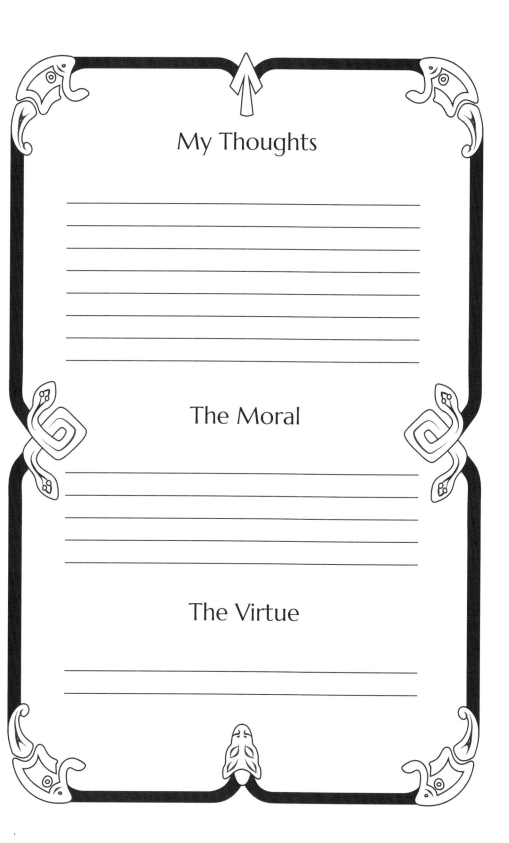

My Thoughts

_____

_____

_____

_____

_____

_____

_____

_____

The Moral

_____

_____

_____

_____

The Virtue

_____

_____

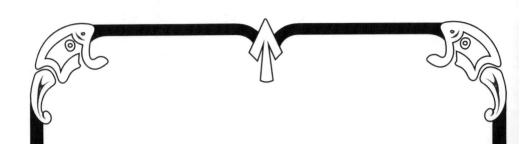

92. To Young Men: To win the love of a woman there are a few things you must do.
Speak kind words to her.
Offer her wealth and a stable home.
Tell her how beautiful she is.
You must court her to win her.

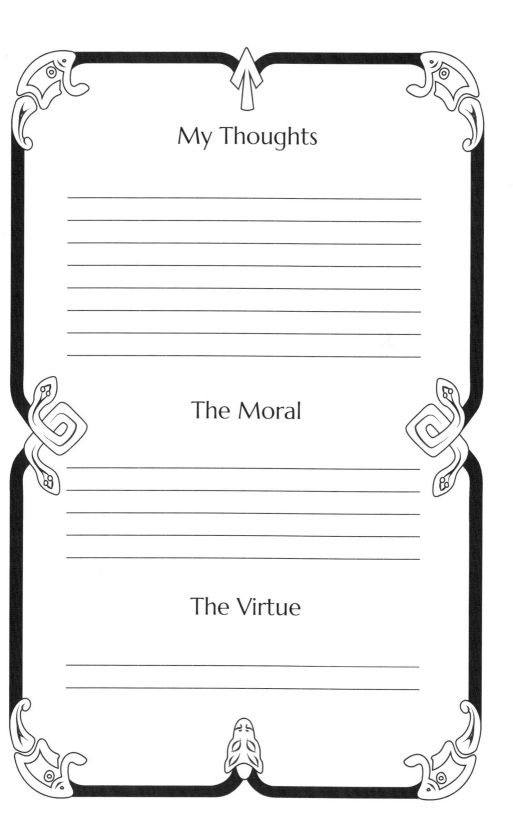

My Thoughts

_____
_____
_____
_____
_____
_____
_____
_____

The Moral

_____
_____
_____
_____

The Virtue

_____
_____

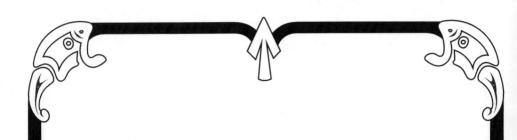

93. You should not blame a person who falls in love for lacking to see the possibility of deceit.
Even the wisest may be fooled by false promises when their hearts rule over their minds.

My Thoughts

_____
_____
_____
_____
_____
_____
_____

The Moral

_____
_____
_____
_____

The Virtue

_____
_____

94. Do not wonder why love can make those who are wise do foolish things.
It happens more often than you might think.
Love makes us do many stupid things.

My Thoughts

_____
_____
_____
_____
_____
_____
_____

The Moral

_____
_____
_____
_____

The Virtue

_____
_____

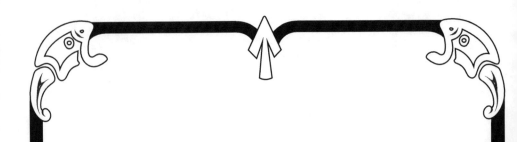

95. Only you may know what is truly in your soul.
No one else can see what is in your heart.
No one else knows your true thoughts.
For those who are wise, there is nothing worse than to not be content.

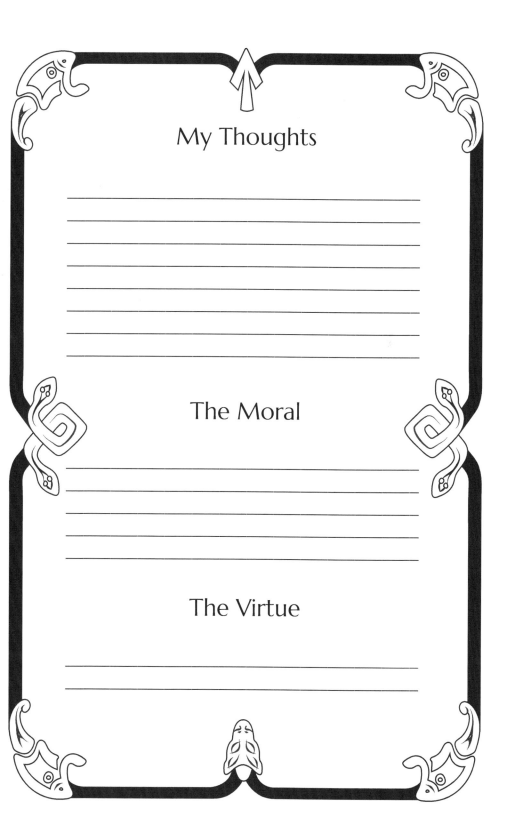

My Thoughts

_____
_____
_____
_____
_____
_____
_____
_____

The Moral

_____
_____
_____
_____
_____

The Virtue

_____
_____

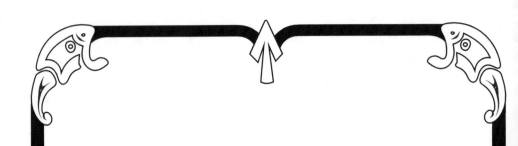

96. I felt this discontent, when once I saw and fell in love with a beautiful woman. With my heart and my soul I loved her yet she did not want me.

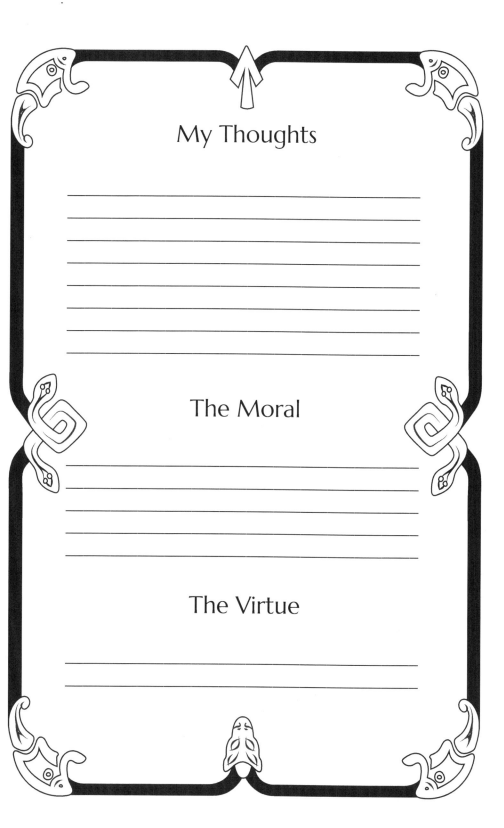

My Thoughts

_____
_____
_____
_____
_____
_____
_____
_____
_____

The Moral

_____
_____
_____
_____
_____

The Virtue

_____
_____

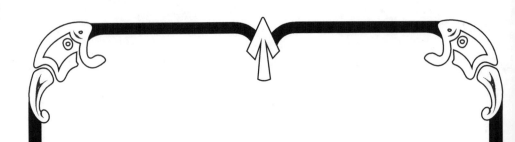

97. I came upon that beautiful woman in the sunlight napping.
In my mind her beauty was all I could think of.
I felt I could find no joy in life if I could not make her mine.

98. "Come in the evening Odin, if you would seek me. Only you and I must know that you wish to make me yours." She said.

99. So I left and waited and thought to myself that all I longed for in my heart and soul would soon be mine. That her love and her heart were now mine.

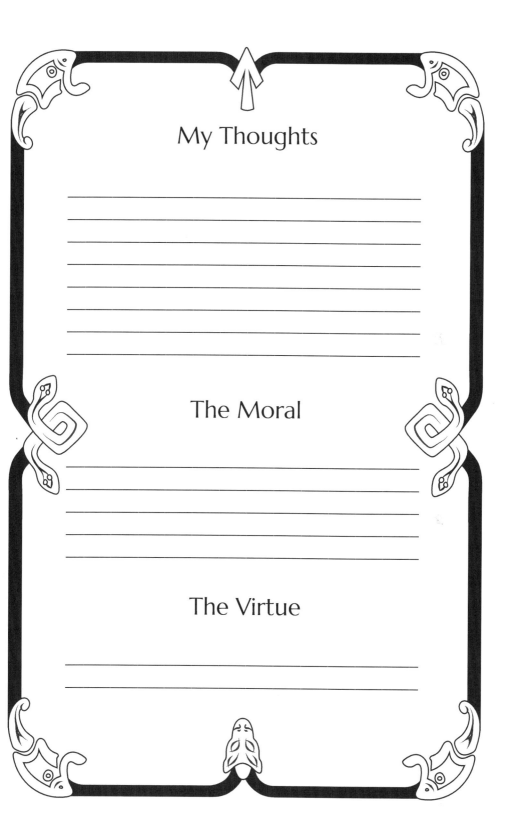

My Thoughts

_____
_____
_____
_____
_____
_____
_____
_____

The Moral

_____
_____
_____
_____
_____

The Virtue

_____
_____

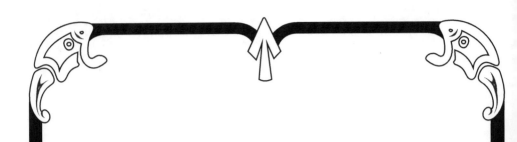

100. But when I returned at night all the guards were awake with lights shining bright.
In sadness I turned away.

101. Yet later near dawn as everyone slept, I crept into her room.
There I did not find her but in her place was a barking dog tied to her bed.

102. Many women are wise to the dishonesty of men and treat them with proper distrust.
I learned this well when I tried to win that beautiful woman with false words.
I did not win her but received only shame and her scorn.

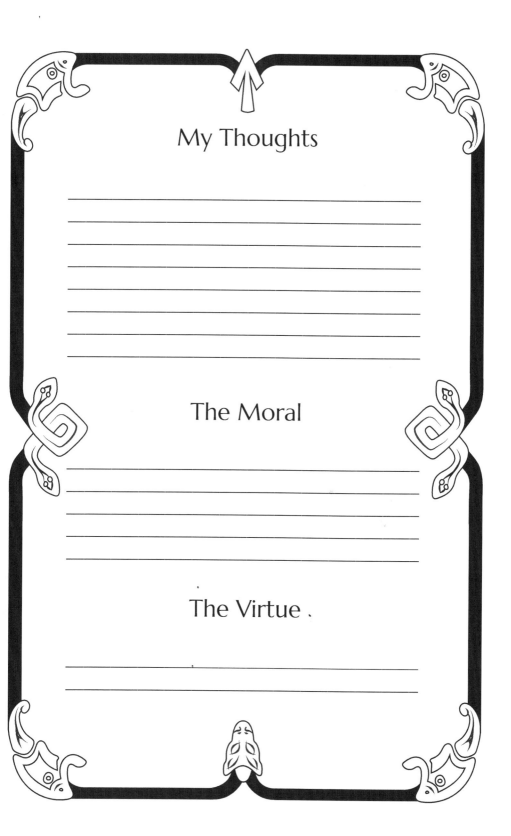

My Thoughts

_____
_____
_____
_____
_____
_____
_____
_____

The Moral

_____
_____
_____
_____
_____

The Virtue

_____
_____

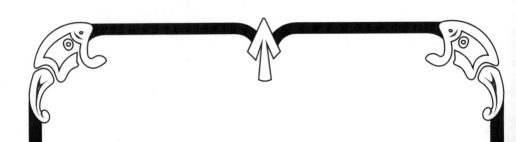

103. At home be cheerful and generous with your guests.
Be careful with your words.
Mindful and proper speech, and a good memory are necessary if you seek to gain wisdom.
One is called a 'fool' or 'stupid' if they have nothing of value to say.
Such is the way of the witless.

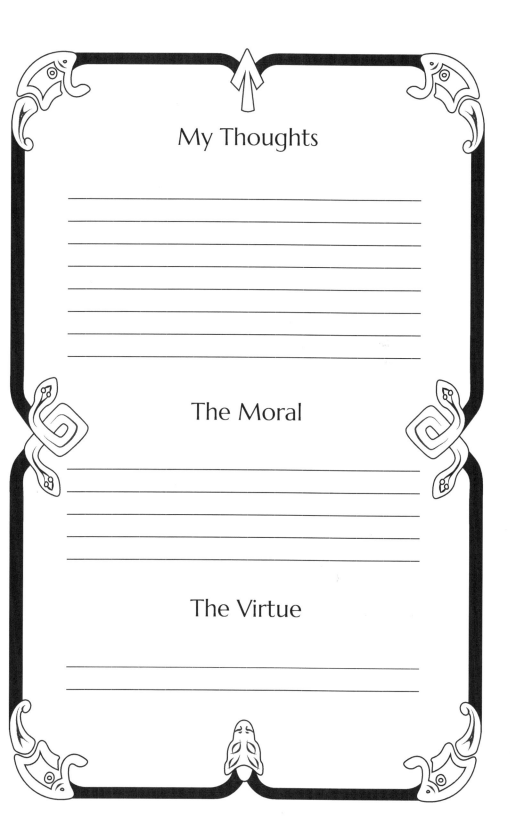

My Thoughts

_____

_____

_____

_____

_____

_____

_____

_____

The Moral

_____

_____

_____

_____

_____

The Virtue

_____

_____

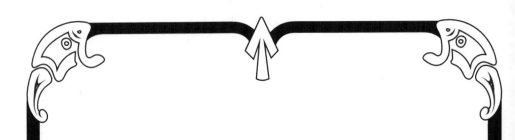

104. Once I sought the Mead of Poetry in the giant Suttung's hall.
Many false words I spoke while my true identity concealed, to enter that hall.

105. In Suttung's hall the fair Gunnlod welcomed me kindly.
She gave me a golden throne and a drink of the mead.
I courted her and made her believe I loved her.
She loved me with all her soul and in return for her kindness I deceived her.

106. I drilled a hole and changed into a snake, through that hole I made my entrance to the home of the giant Suttung.
This is how I risked my life for the Mead of Poetry.

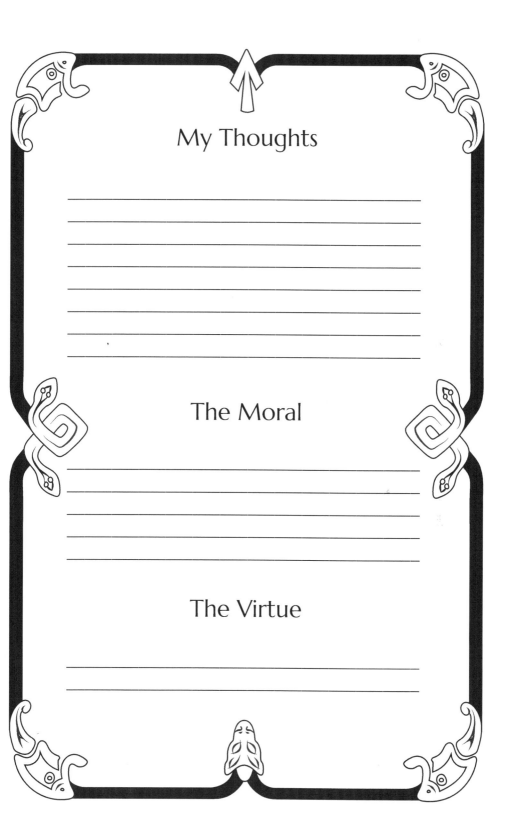

My Thoughts

_____
_____
_____
_____
_____
_____

The Moral

_____
_____
_____
_____

The Virtue

_____
_____

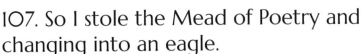

107. So I stole the Mead of Poetry and changing into an eagle.
I fled there with the mead in my belly.
Thus is how the precious mead was shared with the realm of Gods and men.

108. In disguise I fooled Gunnlod and was only able to escape with the mead due to her kindness.

109. The next day the frost giants came to my hall. They called me 'the Evil Doer' and asked if I had returned or if Suttung had found me and killed me.

110. They said, "An oath Odin upon a ring swore and then broke his oath. Who can trust in his troth now? He betrayed Suttung and stole his mead then made dear Gunnlod weep."

This is the story The Mead of Poetry. What did Odin do that was shameful?

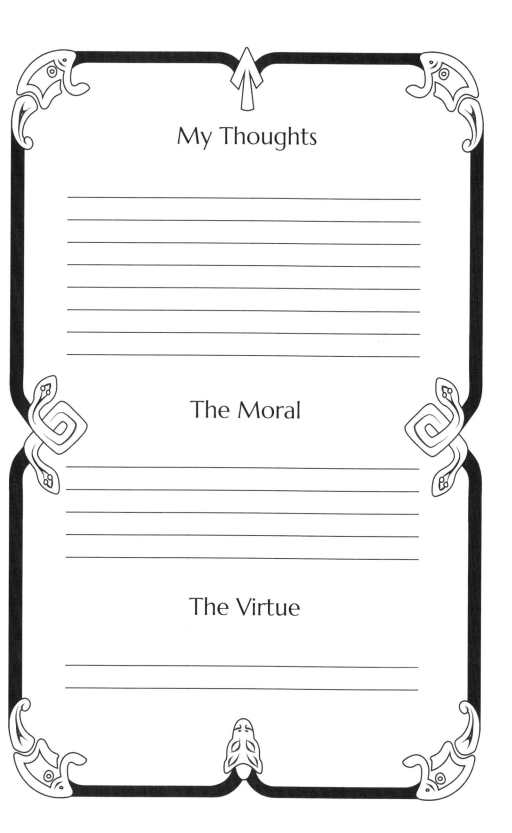

My Thoughts

_____
_____
_____
_____
_____
_____
_____

The Moral

_____
_____
_____
_____

The Virtue

_____
_____

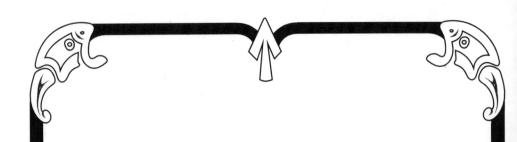

III. Now I will speak of my own wisdom gained by the well of Urd.
I sat silent, I meditated, I watched and listened to the words of men.
Many things I heard.
They spoke of Runes, of reading the Runes, and of the divine.
They gave much wise counsel.
From the seat of the Sage I will share this wisdom with you.

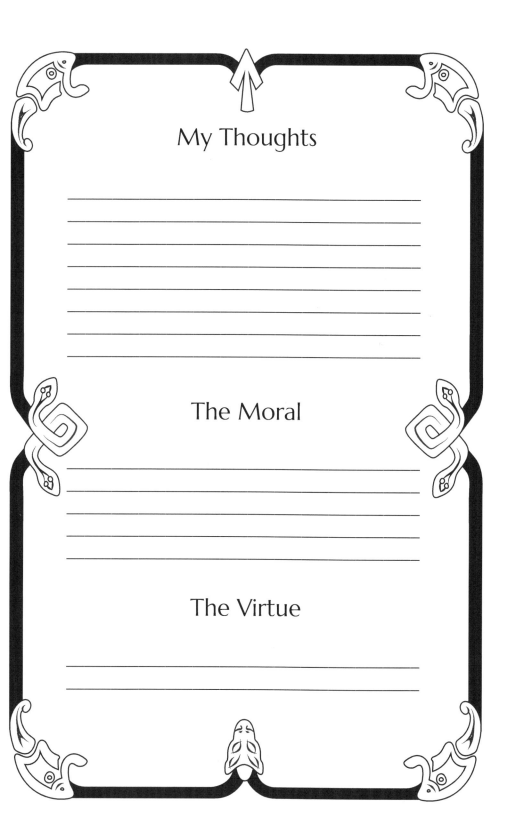

My Thoughts

_____
_____
_____
_____
_____
_____
_____

The Moral

_____
_____
_____
_____
_____

The Virtue

_____
_____

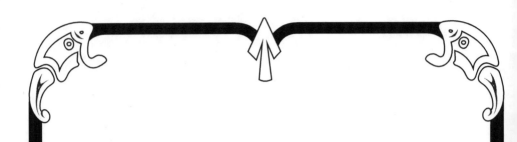

112. I give you this advice, accept my guidance and it will benefit you if you heed it:
Do not get up in the night unless you need to hear something spoken in secret or if you need to use the toilet.

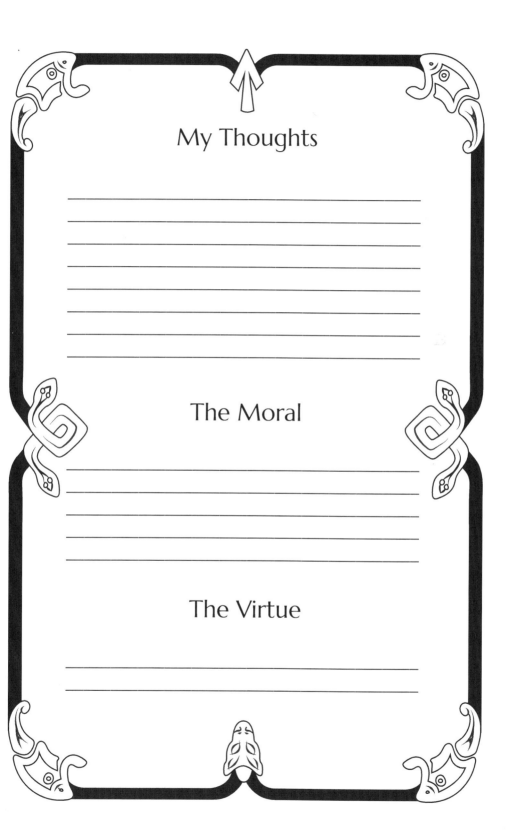

My Thoughts

_____
_____
_____
_____
_____
_____
_____

The Moral

_____
_____
_____
_____

The Virtue

_____
_____

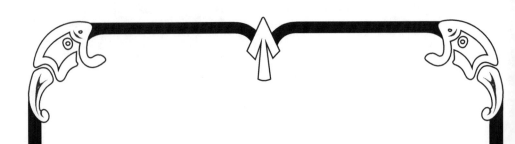

113. I give you this advice, accept my guidance and it will benefit you if you heed it:
Never sleep with a witch who practices black magic, and has perfected the art of cunning.
Never let a woman so evil sway your mind.

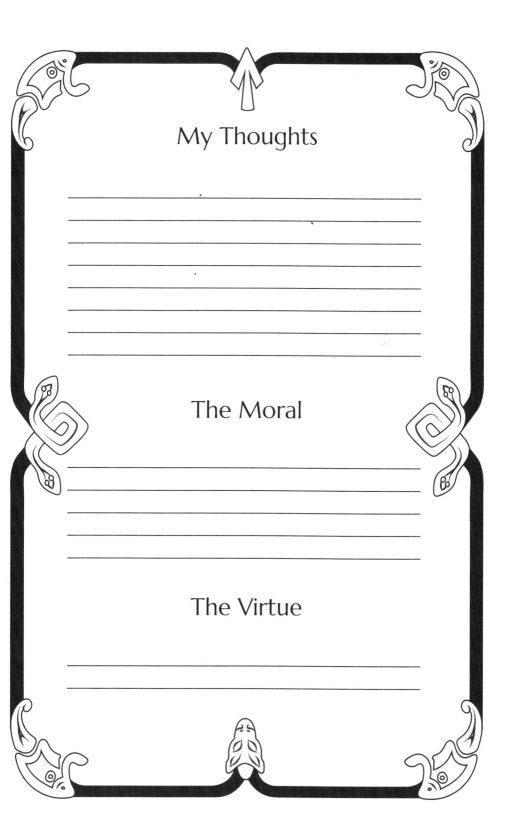

My Thoughts

_____
_____
_____
_____
_____
_____
_____
_____

The Moral

_____
_____
_____
_____

The Virtue

_____
_____

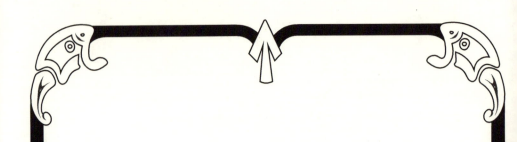

114. If you do not heed my words the wicked woman will charm you with a spell to make you care not for wise counsel or the meetings of men.
You will not care for food and lose all human joys.
Under her spell you will fall into a sorrowful sleep.

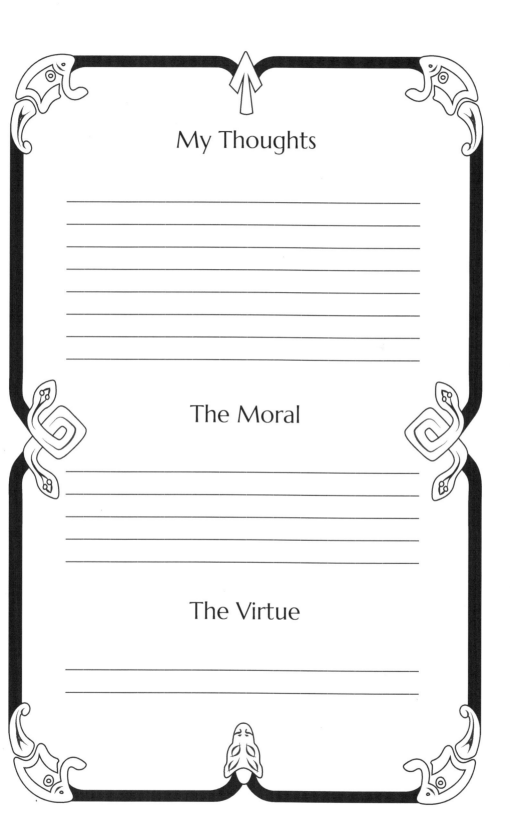

My Thoughts

_____
_____
_____
_____
_____
_____
_____

The Moral

_____
_____
_____
_____

The Virtue

_____
_____

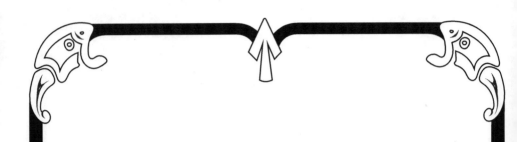

115. I give you this advice, accept my guidance and it will benefit you if you heed it:
Never attempt to steal another's wife or husband nor seek to have their love in secret.

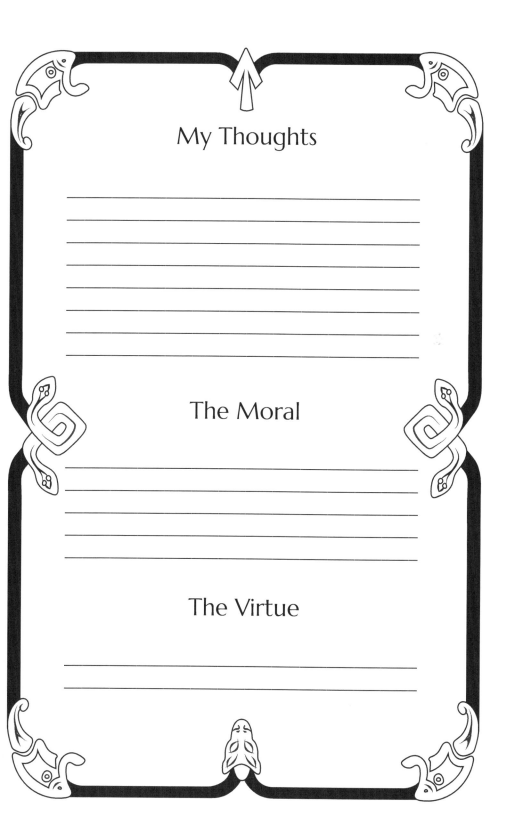

My Thoughts

_____
_____
_____
_____
_____
_____
_____

The Moral

_____
_____
_____
_____

The Virtue

_____
_____

116. I give you this advice, accept my guidance and it will benefit you if you heed it:
If you plan to travel, make sure you are well prepared with food and other necessary provisions.

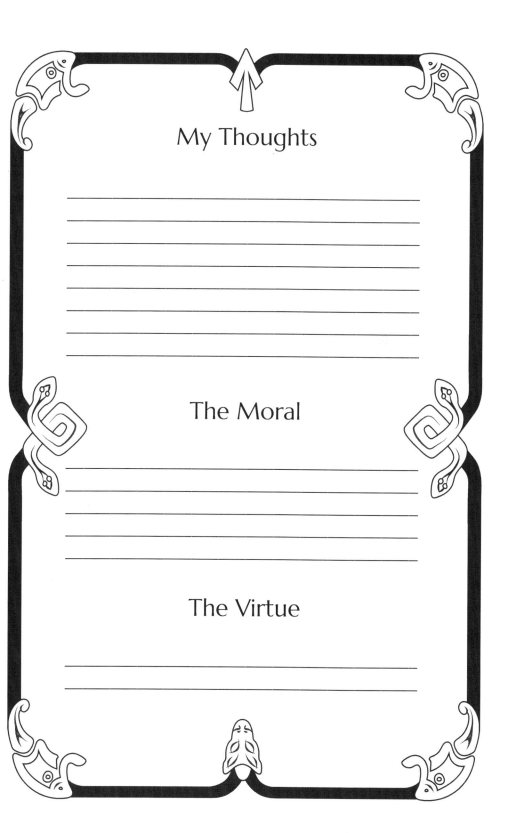

My Thoughts

_____
_____
_____
_____
_____
_____
_____
_____

The Moral

_____
_____
_____
_____

The Virtue

_____
_____

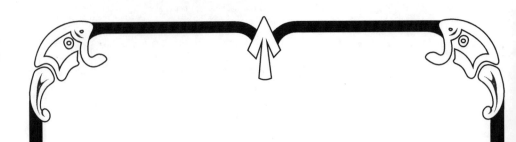

117. I give you this advice, accept my guidance and it will benefit you if you heed it:

Never tell someone who is bad or whom you do not trust, of the misfortunes you have had.

Evil minded people may one day use your words spoken in confidence to harm you.

My Thoughts

_____
_____
_____
_____
_____
_____
_____
_____

The Moral

_____
_____
_____
_____
_____

The Virtue

_____
_____

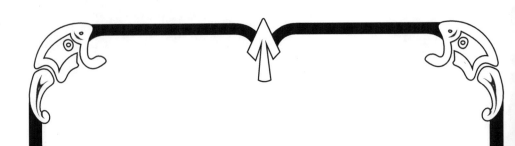

118. I once saw a man killed for a crime he did not commit.
An evil minded woman told lies about him and so by her wickedness an innocent man was sentenced to death.

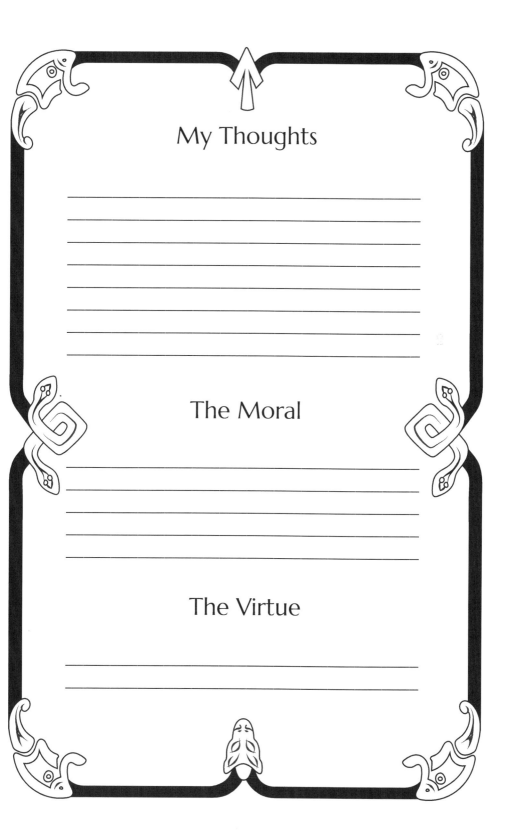

My Thoughts

_____
_____
_____
_____
_____
_____
_____
_____

The Moral

_____
_____
_____
_____

The Virtue

_____
_____

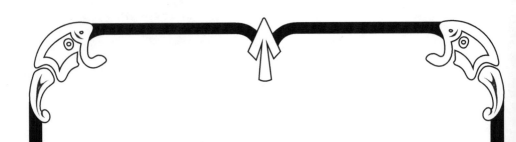

119. I give you this advice, accept my guidance and it will benefit you if you heed it:
If you have a good friend that you know you can trust.
Visit with them often, if you do not your friendship will slowly fade.

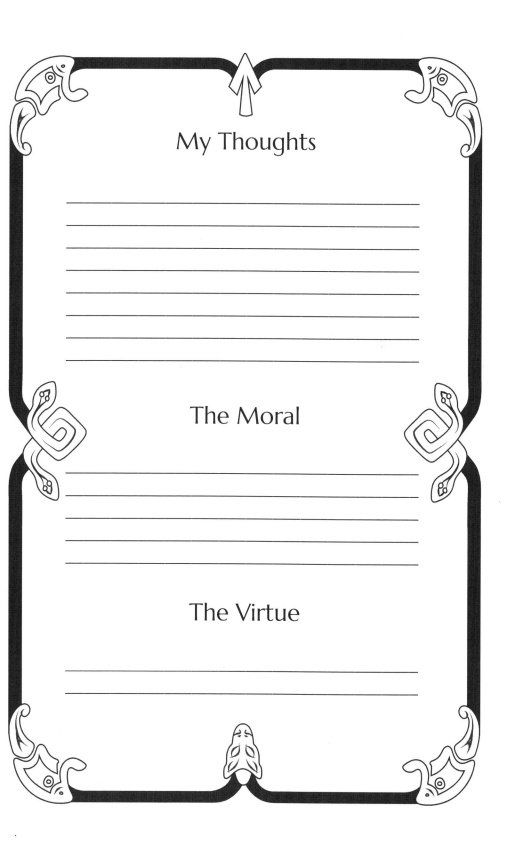

My Thoughts

_____
_____
_____
_____
_____
_____
_____

The Moral

_____
_____
_____
_____

The Virtue

_____
_____

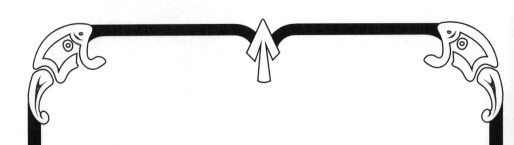

120. I give you this advice, accept my guidance and it will benefit you if you heed it:
Find for yourself a good and wise friend. Speak joyfully with him and learn his healing charms.

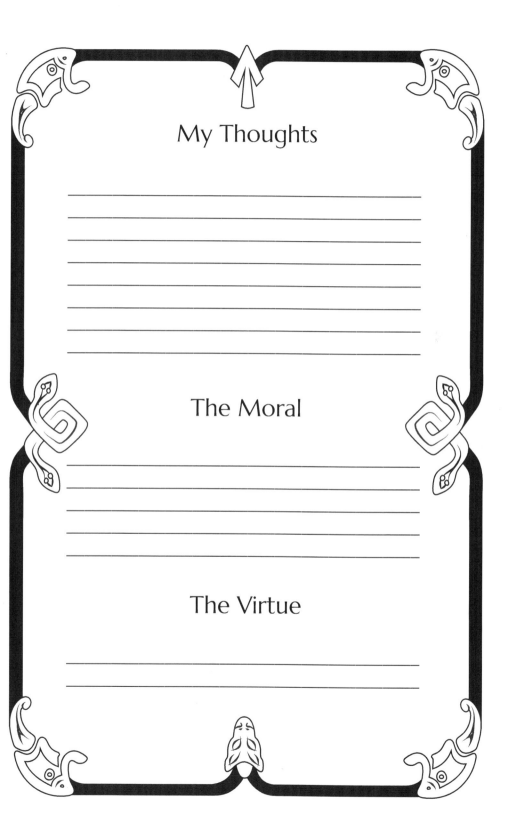

My Thoughts

_____
_____
_____
_____
_____
_____
_____
_____

The Moral

_____
_____
_____
_____
_____

The Virtue

_____
_____

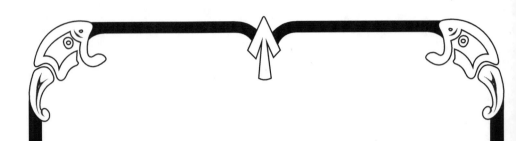

121. I give you this advice, accept my guidance and it will benefit you if you heed it:
Never be the first to cause distrust or a fight with a friend.
Do not lie or be disloyal.
To lose a friend will cause you great sadness.
Life is lonely if you have no one you can tell your thoughts, fears, secrets and desires.

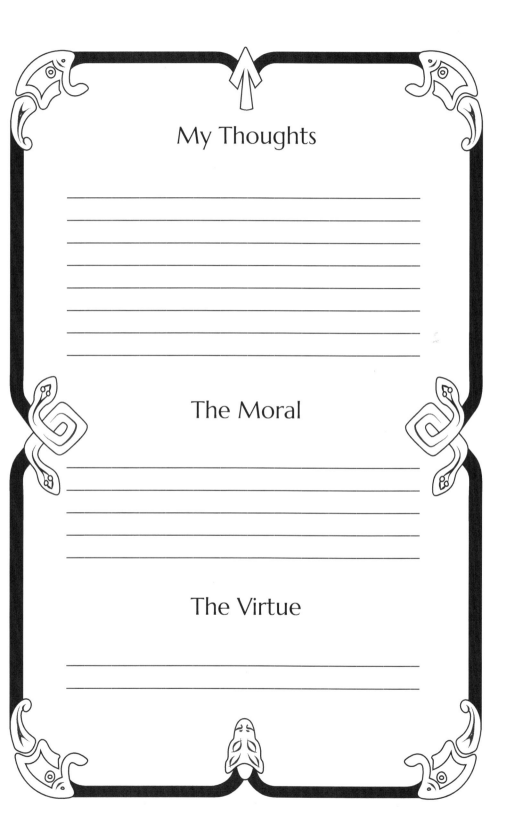

My Thoughts

_____
_____
_____
_____
_____
_____
_____

The Moral

_____
_____
_____
_____

The Virtue

_____
_____

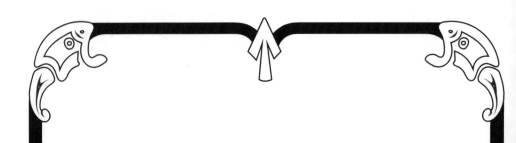

122. I give you this advice, accept my guidance and it will benefit you if you heed it:
Never converse with, argue or debate someone who has no logic, common sense or holds evil thoughts.

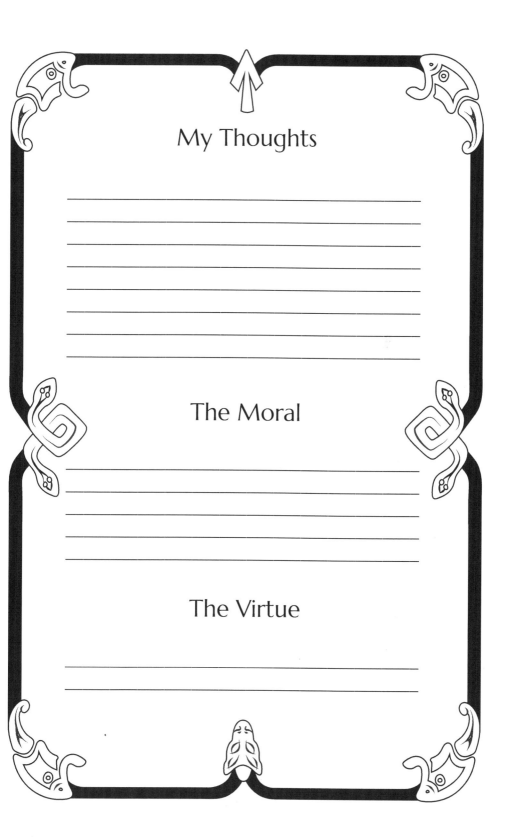

My Thoughts

_____
_____
_____
_____
_____
_____
_____
_____

The Moral

_____
_____
_____
_____
_____

The Virtue

_____
_____

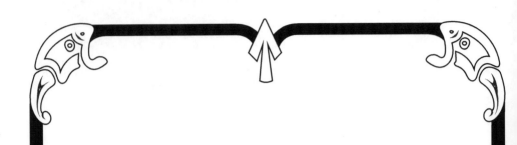

123. I give you this advice, accept my guidance and it will benefit you if you heed it:

From the witless and dangerous person you will never get good things in return.

Rather spend your time with those who are logical, use their mother's wit, and are good hearted.

From these good people you will grow in happiness and learn from each other.

The things they say about you will be good but the evil hearted will only say bad things about you no matter how good you really are.

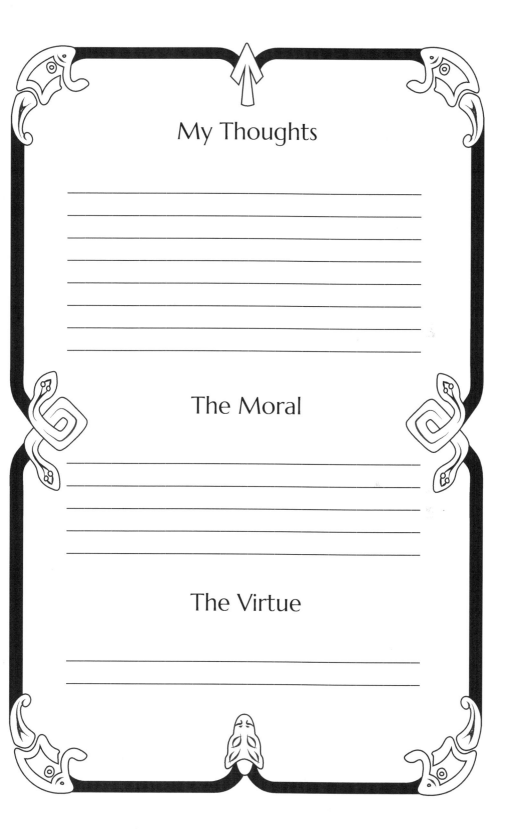

My Thoughts

_____
_____
_____
_____
_____
_____
_____
_____

The Moral

_____
_____
_____
_____

The Virtue

_____
_____

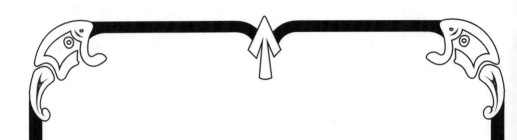

124. I give you this advice, accept my guidance and it will benefit you if you heed it:

There is no truer friendship than one where you can share all of your thoughts with your friend.

There is nothing but a false friendship if you conceal your thoughts and say only kind words to each other.

A true friend will be honest even if their friend may not like what they have to say.

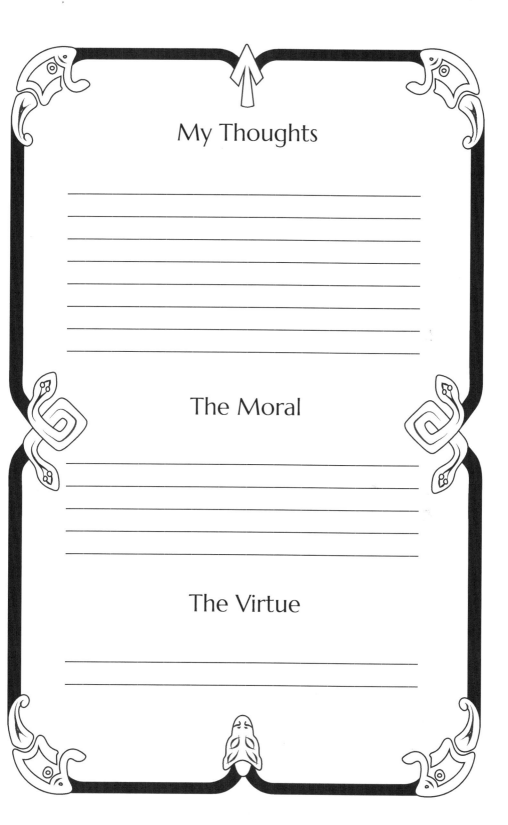

My Thoughts

_____

_____

_____

_____

_____

_____

_____

The Moral

_____

_____

_____

_____

The Virtue

_____

_____

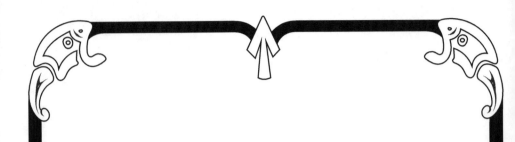

125. I give you this advice, accept my guidance and it will benefit you if you heed it:

Never argue with one who is not as good or wise as you.

Most often the honorable will retreat but the bad and evil minded will always aim to harm you.

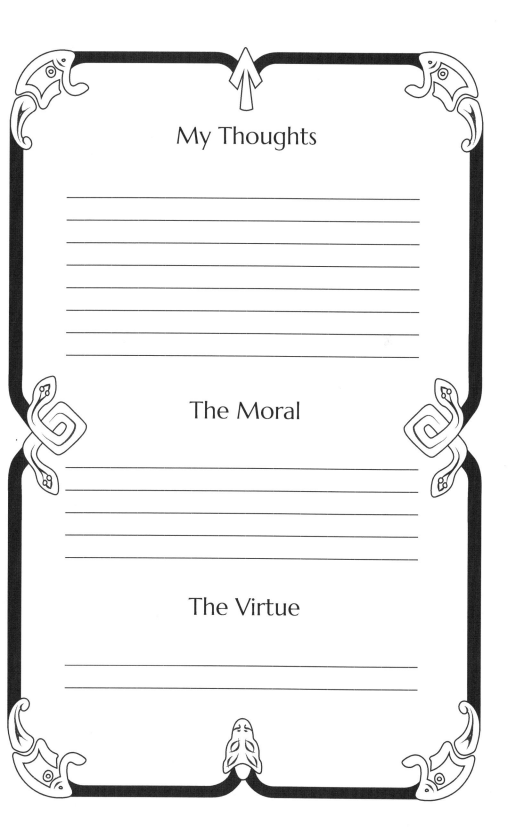

My Thoughts

_____
_____
_____
_____
_____
_____
_____

The Moral

_____
_____
_____
_____

The Virtue

_____
_____

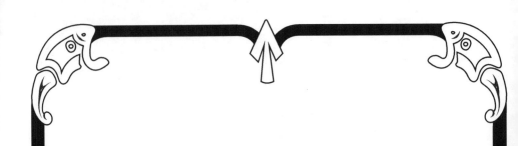

126. I give you this advice, accept my guidance and it will benefit you if you heed it:
Be a crafter for yourself and self sufficient but be wary of making things to be sold or traded to others. If the goods are faulty, people will despise and speak badly about you. If you make goods for others ensure that their quality is high.

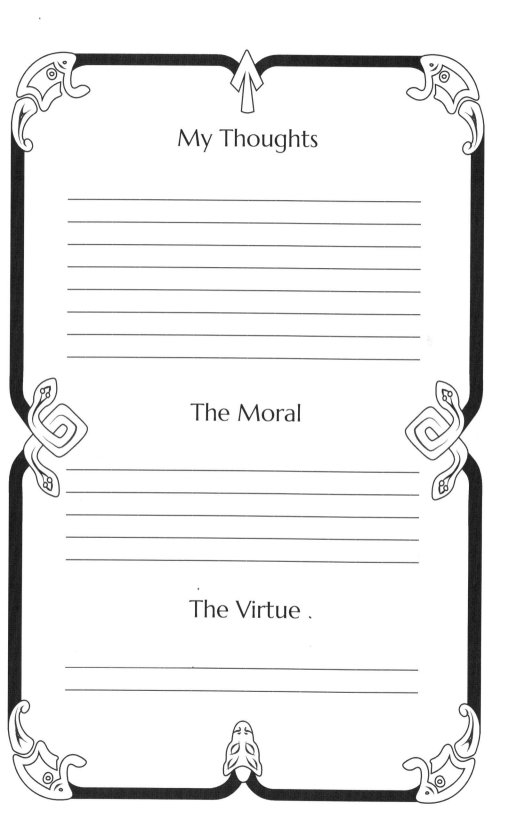

My Thoughts

_____
_____
_____
_____
_____
_____
_____
_____

The Moral

_____
_____
_____
_____
_____

The Virtue

_____
_____

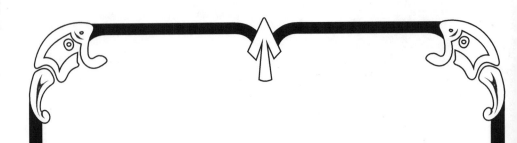

127. I give you this advice, accept my guidance and it will benefit you if you heed it:
If evil you see then say what it is and never give your enemies the chance to harm you. Even if you do not seek a war from your enemy never enter an oath with them or trust them.
They will not honor the oath even if you do.

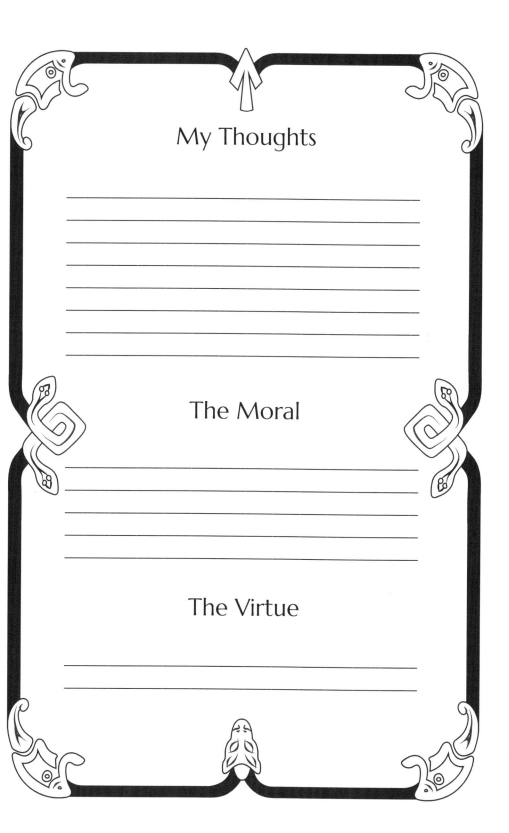

My Thoughts

_____
_____
_____
_____
_____
_____
_____

The Moral

_____
_____
_____
_____

The Virtue

_____
_____

128. I give you this advice, accept my guidance and it will benefit you if you heed it:
Do not take happiness from doing bad things or from evil.
Instead take joy and happiness from the good in the world and in doing good yourself.

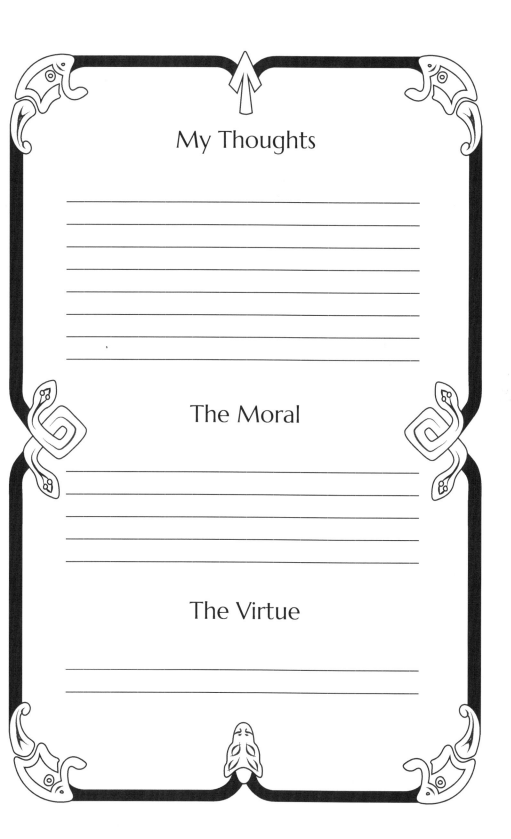

My Thoughts

_____

_____

_____

_____

_____

_____

_____

The Moral

_____

_____

_____

_____

The Virtue

_____

_____

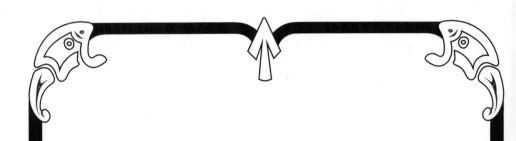

129. I give you this advice, accept my guidance and it will benefit you if you heed it:
Keep focused on your task when in battle and don't look at what is happening around you.
The chaos will make you lose your senses and fear will control you.

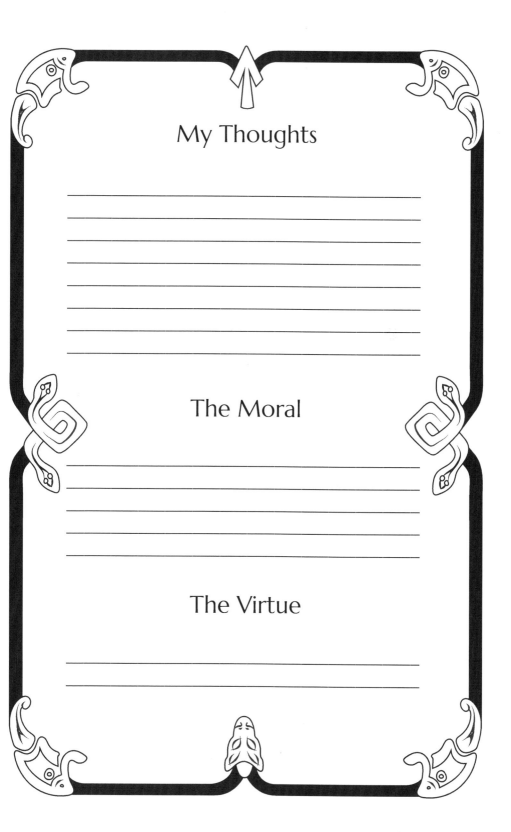

My Thoughts

_____

_____

_____

_____

_____

_____

_____

The Moral

_____

_____

_____

_____

The Virtue

_____

_____

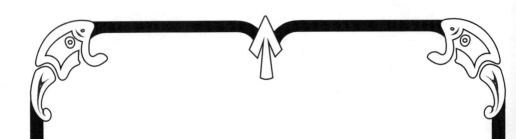

130. I give you this advice, accept my guidance and it will benefit you if you heed it:

If you want a good and kind girl to fall in love with you, then you must say kind things and make promises to her that you will keep.

Only good will come to you for being kind and honorable to a good woman.

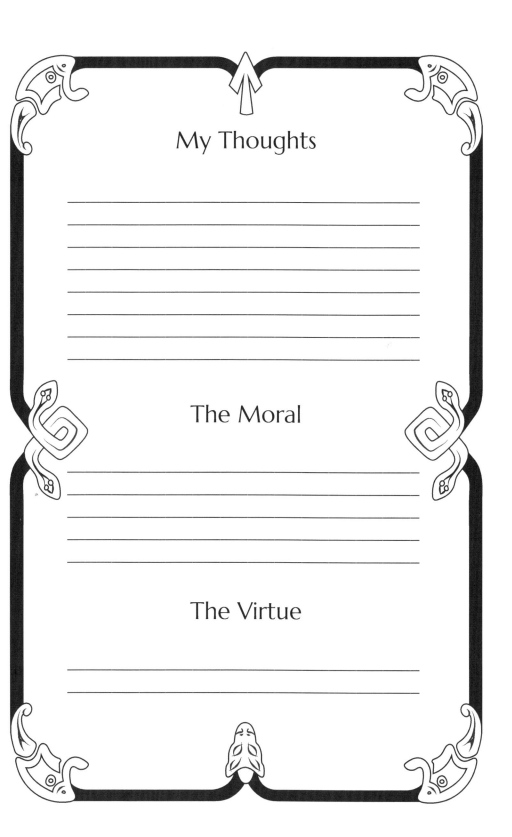

My Thoughts

_____
_____
_____
_____
_____
_____
_____
_____

The Moral

_____
_____
_____
_____
_____

The Virtue

_____
_____

131. I give you this advice, accept my guidance and it will benefit you if you heed it:

Always be prepared for anything you may one day face. But never let yourself be controlled by fear or worry.

Be careful most with drinking alcohol, with another persons wife or husband, and always keep watch that thieves and evil minded people do not take advantage of you.

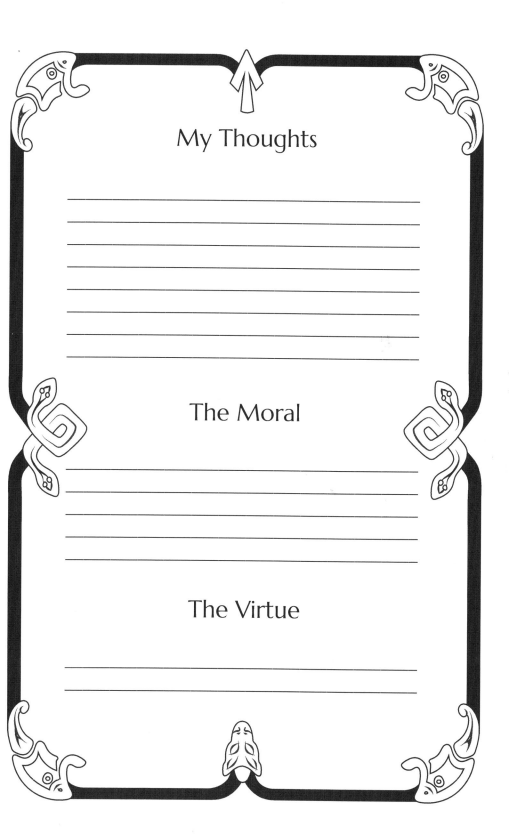

My Thoughts

_____
_____
_____
_____
_____
_____
_____

The Moral

_____
_____
_____
_____

The Virtue

_____
_____

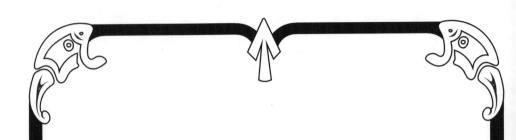

132. I give you this advice, accept my guidance and it will benefit you if you heed it:
Never tease, make fun of or insult a guest or a stranger.

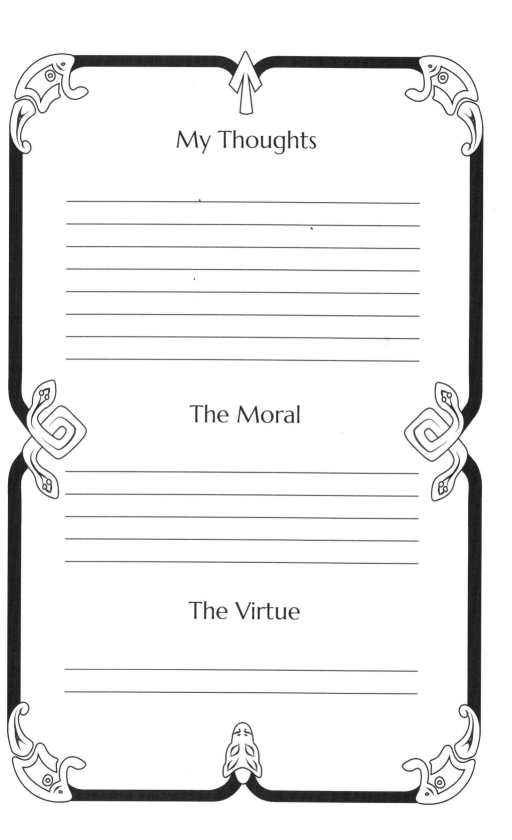

My Thoughts

The Moral

The Virtue

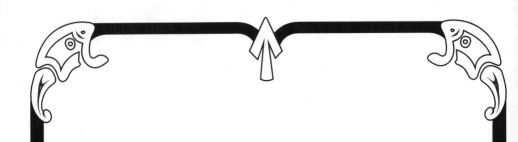

133. I give you this advice, accept my guidance and it will benefit you if you heed it:

Most often than not you do not know what kind of person another is.

No one is so good that they have never made mistakes and no one is so bad that there is nothing good they have ever done.

We are all capable of doing good and evil things.

It is our choices that determine what kind of person we are.

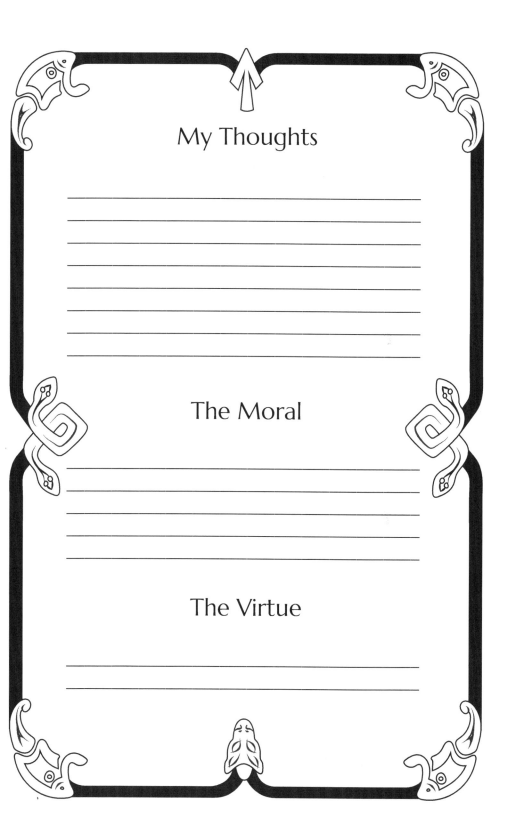

My Thoughts

_____
_____
_____
_____
_____
_____
_____
_____

The Moral

_____
_____
_____
_____

The Virtue

_____
_____

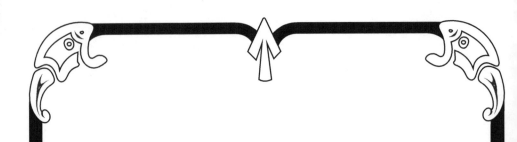

134. I give you this advice, accept my guidance and it will benefit you if you heed it:

Never disregard, ignore, or disrespect the words spoken by the elders.

Though they are old, they have experienced a lot and gained much wisdom.

Their words of common sense can teach and help guide you.

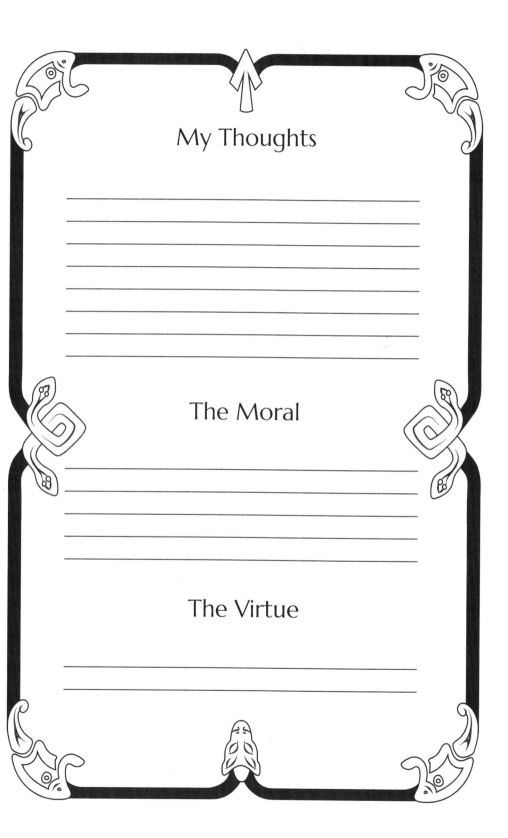

My Thoughts

_____

_____

_____

_____

_____

_____

_____

_____

The Moral

_____

_____

_____

_____

The Virtue

_____

_____

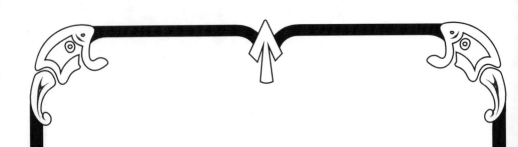

135. I give you this advice, accept my guidance and it will benefit you if you heed it:
Be kind and respectful to a guest.
Never throw them out unless their own behavior necessitates it.
Treat the poor and in need well.
They will regard you highly and so too will others if you follow the rules of hospitality.

Be wary of welcoming people into your home however. The rules of hospitality only apply if he who enters your home also follows them.

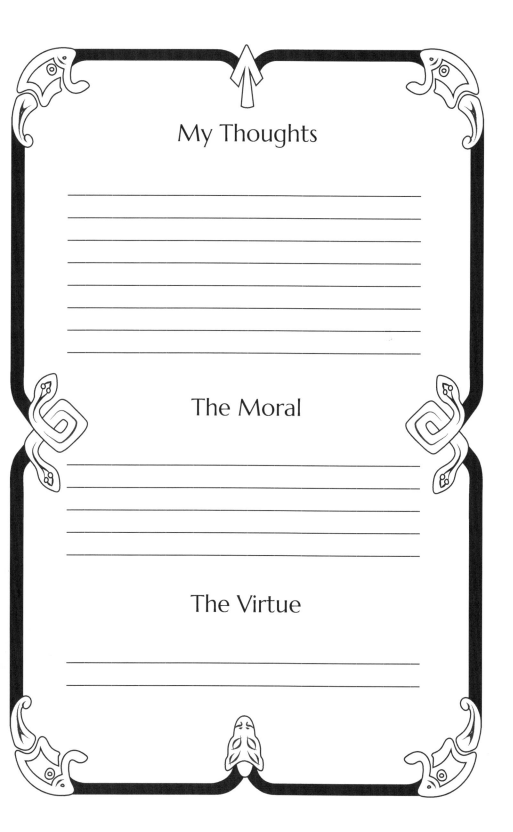

My Thoughts

_____
_____
_____
_____
_____
_____
_____

The Moral

_____
_____
_____
_____
_____

The Virtue

_____
_____

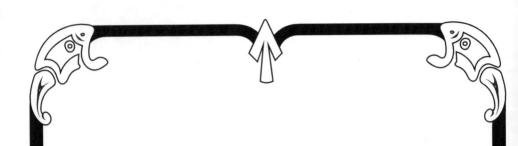

136. I give you this advice, accept my guidance and it will benefit you if you heed it:
Even hospitality has its limits.
Do not overextend yourself for other people.
They will begin to expect from you the things that were given in kindness.

Remember we cannot save the world with our charity. If we give everything away we ourselves become poor. We can close our door and still be kind and courteous to everyone we meet.

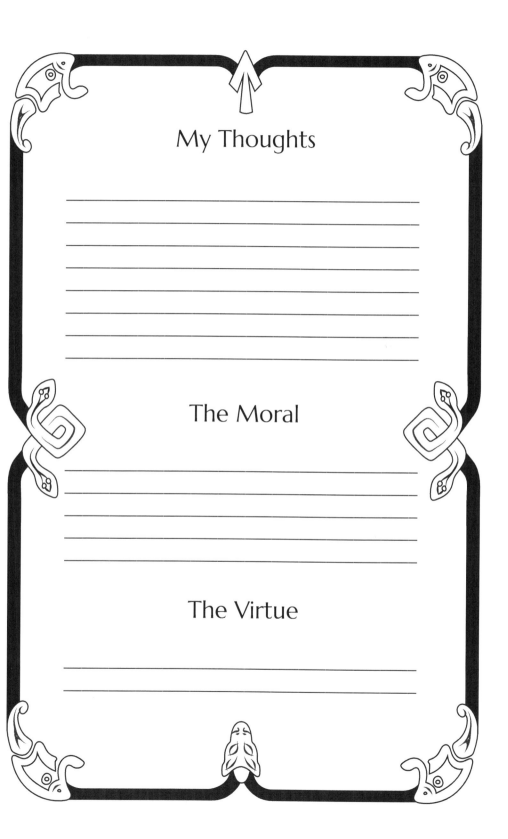

My Thoughts

_____

_____

_____

_____

_____

_____

_____

The Moral

_____

_____

_____

_____

The Virtue

_____

_____

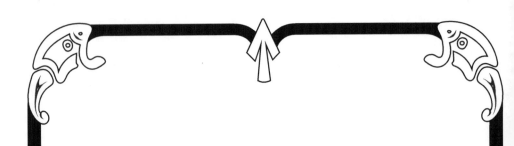

137. I give you this advice, accept my guidance and it will benefit you if you heed it:

List of charms: If you drink alcohol then seek the earth the earth cures the drunk,

Invoke fire for sickness, use oak to heal constipation and stomach pains,

Use the head of wheat against magic, use rye against family problems,

Invoke the moon for hatred, use the snake against snake bites, and runes against evil.

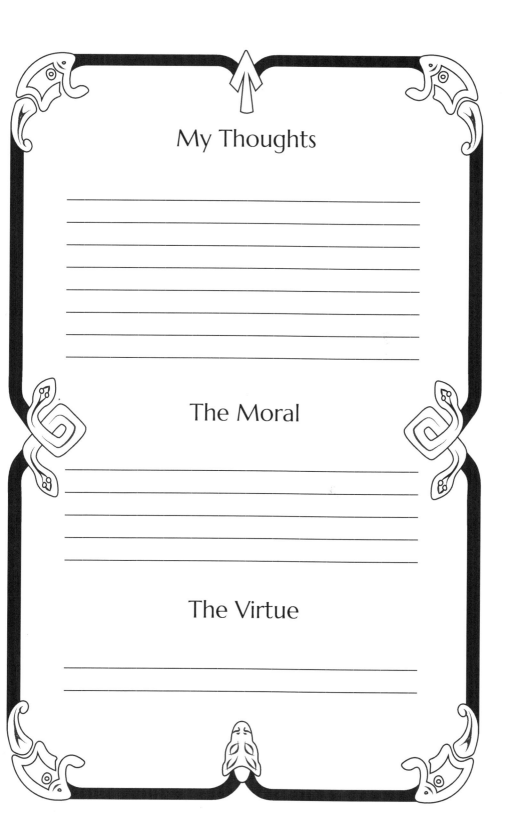

My Thoughts

_____
_____
_____
_____
_____
_____
_____

The Moral

_____
_____
_____
_____
_____

The Virtue

_____
_____

THE END

Thus ends the part of the Havamal that deals in advice on morals and virtues. The remaining section is about charms so it has not been included here.

This book is not intended to be a literal translation of the Havamal. Instead it seeks to pull the morals from the text to better understand them.

I implore you to seek out the various poetic translations if you are interested in seeing how others before me have interpreted the Havamal.

You can use this book as a companion to The Study Havamal also released by Huginn & Muninn Publishing which includes the original Old Norse and three English language translations.

Watch for the second book in the
Coming of Age series available in 2021

For more books on Asatru, Odinism,
Germanic, Celtic & Slavic Heathenry
Please visit us on the web at:

www.huginnandmuninn.net

Huginn & Muninn Publishing

Made in the USA
Middletown, DE
25 May 2025